Serger Sewing Basics

Have a few minutes? You can create a poufy ruffle and attach it to a pillow, insert a satin ribbon in heirloom lace, add a fun binding to clothing or home decor, and piece a pretty quilt top with fancy decorative threads. All you need to do these things and more is something you may have sitting under a cover of dust in your sewing room or in a box in your closet—or maybe it is a new purchase. No matter where it is, armed with this book and your serger you will soon be entering a whole new world of creativity—a world that will put you at center stage when family and friends see what you have made!

Rose Garden Kitchen Set, **page 56**

Throughout the pages of this book, you'll learn the keys to successful serger sewing. You will get to know your serger, how and why it works, and what it can do for you. You'll learn the basics of setting up the stitches and how to use them, as well as how to troubleshoot and make adjustments needed to achieve the perfect stitch. You'll also learn about tension, stitch length, cutting width, differential feed, stitching with and without the cutting blades, creating seams, finishing edges and many other basic techniques.

Best of all, once you've learned the basics, then it's time to explore your machine's creative potential. Combine your imagination with the lush yarns and decorative threads available today. At the back of this book, you'll find 13 projects designed for practicing your newfound knowledge and skills. Now is the time to let your serger inspire creative endeavors you never dreamed of before!

Table of Contents

Chapter One: Making Friends With Your Serger

What can your serger do for you? A lot! Maybe more than you can even imagine once you get to know how it works and its potential for creativity.

Sergers have come a long way since they were introduced to the home-sewing market in 1969. Today's machines are capable of multiple stitches and uses that still include, but surpass, the basic 2- or 3-thread overlock. Depending on the model, your machine may accommodate five or more threads, have special attachments and even include a computerized stitch advisor.

The basic function of a serger is really quite simple—it simultaneously sews a seam while it trims the fabric edges and encases them in neat, even stitches. Also, like a sewing machine, it has adjustable stitch length and width, adjustable presser foot tensions, and the capability of working with a variety of needles and threads. While there are many functions that a computerized sewing/embroidery machine can do that a serger can't, there also are many functions and techniques exclusive to the serger—making it a wonderful companion in your sewing room.

Unlike a sewing machine, sergers actually cut the fabric as they sew—stitching with a system of loopers and needles rather than with a bobbin and needle. Newer sergers also feature a differential feed system that eliminates stretching and puckering that can happen when you are stitching.

With a serger, you can create reversible projects with ease. The overlock finishes edges with stitches that look equally nice from each side, and the flat lock features decorative stitches on one side of the fabric and a ladder stitch on the opposite side.

It's easy to hem linens with rolled edges or to hem knits with the cover stitch. And of course, adding decorative embellishments to your serger projects is part of the fun. With the wide array of decorative threads available, you can create amazing accents for both the surface and edges of your fabrics.

Meet Your Machine

The first step in befriending your machine is to understand its features and how to use and control them. Take the time to familiarize yourself with the parts of your serger and how they work by reading your manual and comparing it to your machine. The following illustration is a generalized look at today's serger parts (Figure 1.1).

A) Chain Stitch Looper (Part of the Lower Looper System)

B) Feed Dogs

C) Hand Wheel

D) Lower Knife

E) Lower Looper

F) Lower Looper Tensions

G) Needles

H) Needle Thread Tensions

I) Presser Foot

J) Spool Holders for Thread

K) Thread Guide

L) Upper Looper Tension

M) Upper Knife

N) Upper Looper

O) Front Cover

P) Stitch Finger

Q) Differential Feed

R) Stitch Length

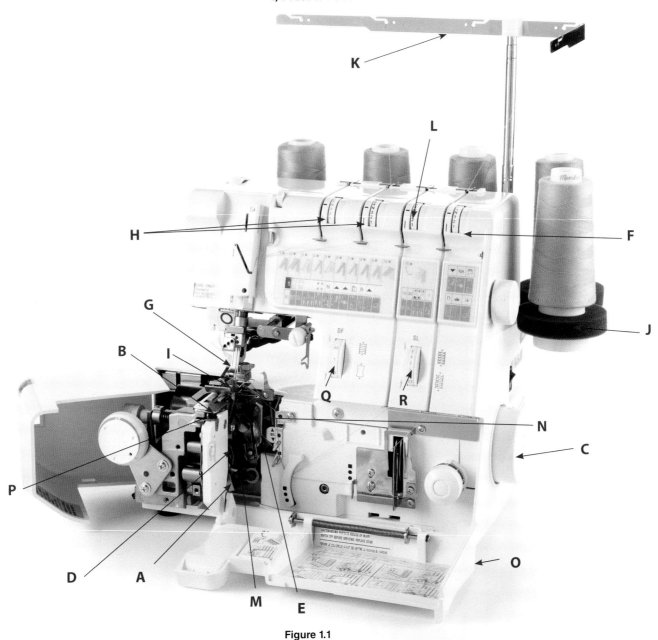

Figure 1.1

The Basic Overlock Stitch

Unlike a sewing machine that forms stitches with a needle and bobbin, the basic overlock is formed with needles and loopers. As the fabric is fed through the machine, the upper looper forms a loop that lies on top of the fabric, while the lower looper forms a loop that lies underneath the fabric, encasing the edge. The needle(s) thread catches and secures the interlocking loops to the fabric; they also lock at the fabric edge.

Mastering the Controls

Even if your serger has a computerized stitch advisor that shows you the exact settings for each stitch, it's important to know how the controls work and what they do so you can make adjustments when needed. Different fabrics and threads react differently to serger stitching, so you will very often be making adjustments in order to get that perfect stitch for your project. Once you get to know your serger, you won't be afraid to touch those tension dials or to make other adjustments. In fact, that will become part of the fun of serging!

Cutting Width & Stitch Width

One of the best time-saving features of a serger is the cutting system. It trims the fabric with two blades—one upper and one lower—that work like scissors to cut the fabric. On most sergers, the upper blade can be moved out of the way for cover stitches and some flat-lock applications.

The distance between the upper blade and the needle closest to the blade is the cutting width, or the width of the fabric edge that will be finished with the serged stitches. It is different than the seam allowance, which is the distance between the needle and the edge of the fabric. Usually when

Some bulky or heavy-weight fabrics can be difficult to cut with your serger, even with sharp blades and a wider cutting width. To get a smooth cut started, use scissors to trim the width that will be cut away for the first inch or two of the edge. This enables the feed dogs and presser foot to grab the fabric and stitch a straight seam at the beginning. You will also want to sew at a slower speed.

Sharp blades are important for a clean-cut edge. Plan to replace the blades when they begin to dull. Man-made fabrics, like polyester and tricot, cause your blades to dull more quickly than natural fibers.

serging seams, part of the seam allowance will be cut off. On some sergers, the cutting blades may be adjustable to increase or decrease the cutting width. This may be a setting on a computerized machine, or you may need to manually move the blades. Consult your owner's manual to see if you have this option and how to use it.

One way to adjust the stitch width is by changing the needle position. Use the left needle only for a wide stitch and the right needle only for a narrow stitch. Consult your machine manual to see if it might also have controls to adjust the stitch width.

Another way to adjust the stitch width is by moving the stitch finger, which is where the loopers are placing the thread to form the stitch (Figure 1.3). Depending on your model, there may be a lever to adjust the stitch finger, or you may need to move it manually.

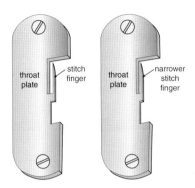

Figure 1.3

Decreased length

You will want to adjust the cutting width for some fabrics, certain stitches and to correct tension problems.

Tips for Stitch Width

If loops hang off the edge of the fabric, the stitch width is wider than the cutting width. Widen the cutting width or decrease the stitch width.

If the loops make indentations along the fabric edge, the cutting width is wider than the stitch width. Decrease the cutting width or widen the stitch width.

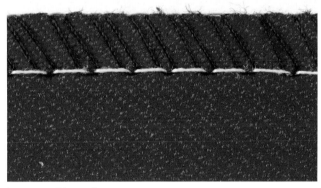

Increased length

Tips for Success

Sometimes adjusting the stitch width or length is all that's needed for perfect tension. As a general rule, use a longer stitch length and wider stitch width on heavy or bulky fabrics, and a shorter stitch length and narrower stitch width on lightweight or sheer fabrics.

Stitch Length

Like sewing machine stitches, the length of serger stitches can be adjusted. Simply set the stitch length on your machine as you would for a sewing machine. A normal overlock stitch length is 2.5mm on medium-weight woven fabric. Depending on your machine, you may be able to adjust the length from 0.8mm for rolled edges to 5mm for cover stitches. As a rule of thumb, you will want to decrease the length for lightweight or sheer fabrics and some metallic threads, and increase it for heavier fabrics and threads.

Differential Feed & Presser Foot Adjustment

A differential feed system has two sets of feed dogs—one in front of the other. The front set of feed dogs feeds the fabric under the presser foot, and the back set feeds it out of the serger. When you adjust the differential feed system, it sets the front set of feed dogs to feed more or less fabric under the foot, and to the back set of feed dogs. The uneven feeding gathers or stretches the fabric as it's serged, eliminating unwanted puckers or distortion. You can also use this feature to intentionally gather an edge or stretch it to create a lettuce-leaf edge.

Check your manual for specifics on adjusting the differential feed system. On most machines, the fabric is gathered more as the differential feed number is increased, and the fabric is stretched more as the number is decreased.

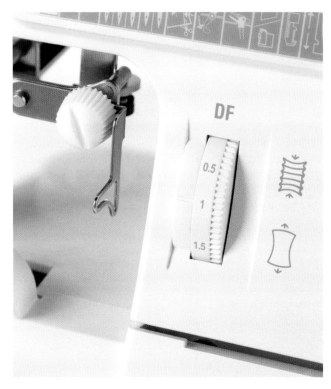

If your serger does not have a differential feed system, you can compensate for fabric weight and stretch by adjusting the presser foot pressure. A lighter pressure will allow heavier and stretchy fabric to pass between the feed dogs and presser foot, easily leaving a smoother seam. Refer to your owner's manual for more details.

Threading for Success

Many people dread threading a serger and cringe at the thought of a thread breaking. True, it is more complicated than threading your sewing machine, but it really isn't that difficult. The most important thing to remember is that *the loopers and needles need to be threaded in the correct order* to stitch properly. Some models thread themselves or can be threaded in any order, but *most have specific requirements*. Most manufacturers recommend that you thread the upper looper first, and then the lower looper and needles—in that order. Refer to the owner's manual for your model. Not threading your

machine in the correct order will result in crossed threads that will break or cause a jam when you begin stitching.

Use serger tweezers as needed to help position the threads as you thread each looper and needle. It's also important to place all threads under the back of the foot before you begin stitching to ensure your beginning stitches sew correctly. The loopers and needles on a serger move at the same time making it easy for threads that aren't anchored under the foot to pop out of the needle or looper eye.

Don't despair if you have to rethread for some reason. Breaking a thread is bound to happen, and you will also need to change thread colors. Once you know how to thread your machine, it will be an easy task. If you are just changing colors it isn't necessary to completely rethread the machine. You can "tie on" the new thread to that which is already in your loopers and needles. Clip the threads close to the cones and place the new colors on the thread stand. Tie the new threads to the ends of the old threads with a tight square knot,

Tips for Success

Make sure the threads are securely between the plates in the tension guides. If they aren't, it will appear that the tension needs adjusting.

To have a better understanding of the threading system, use a different color thread for each looper and needle. When you stitch a sample, you will see which thread came from each spool and where that thread appears to make the particular stitch. This will also help you make any tension adjustments because you will be able to easily identify the problem looper or needle.

Sergers sew fast! Some specialty threads may slip from the cone or spool or tangle as you serge. To prevent this, cover the cone or spool with a thread net.

leaving a 2- to 3-inch tail on the knot. Adjust the tension to zero on all needles and loopers, and slowly and carefully pull the threads through the guides. Knotted threads will go completely through the loopers, but stop and cut the knots when they reach the needles and then rethread the needle. Attempting to pull a knot through the needle may bend or break it.

This also works for some thread breaks. Depending on where the break occurs, you may have to rethread that looper or needle. When rethreading, make sure the threads are still placed in the correct order. For example, if the looper thread breaks, the needle thread(s) must be removed before rethreading the looper.

Tension Relief

Next to improper threading, tension is the cause of most stitch formation problems—and the cause of most headaches—for serger users. Like threading, once you understand the effects of tension, it's easier to see how to make adjustments. When the looper and needle threads all form the stitch correctly, the tension is referred to as "balanced."

Most sergers have numbered tension dials, which makes tension adjustment relatively easy. Similar to your sewing machine, tension is adjusted for different weights of fabric. As a general rule: The more loft or thickness of the fabric, the looser the tension should be for needles and loopers. Fine or sheer fabrics need a tighter tension in both needles and loopers.

On a balanced 3- or 4-thread overlock, the upper looper threads form an "S" shape on the top of the fabric and lock with the lower looper thread along the edge. The lower looper thread should form a "V" for 3-thread stitching or a "Y" for 4-thread stitching on the underside of the fabric and lock with the upper looper thread along the edge.

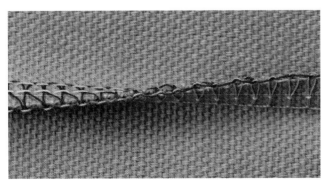

Balanced 4-thread Overlock.

Tension Basics

Set the needle tensions first, and then the looper tensions. The reason for setting the needle tensions first is that the stitch formation is a combination of threads looped together. If one thread is too tight or loose, another thread can compensate for that tightness or looseness. Thus, for the best-looking seams possible, always adjust the left needle tension first because it affects the edges of the looper threads. Only adjust one tension dial at a time to balance tension.

Adjusting Tension on Overlock

The appearance of overlock is very similar when the upper looper tension is too tight and the lower looper tension is too loose. It also is very similar when the upper tension is too loose and the lower tension is too loose. Examine the stitch closely to see if you can determine whether it is being pulled or is simply too loose. Experiment with adjustments until the stitch is balanced.

The upper looper tension is too tight if the stitches are pulling the lower looper thread to the top of the fabric.

Upper looper tension is too tight.

The lower looper tension is too tight if the stitches are pulling the upper looper thread to the underside of the fabric.

To correct, turn the corresponding tension dial to the left to loosen the looper tension.

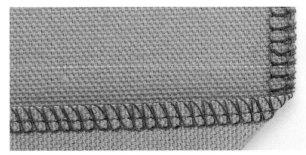

Lower looper tension is too tight.

The upper looper tension is too loose if the threads are wrapping around the edge to the underside or extending off the edge.

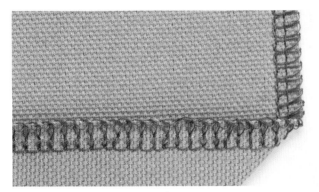

Upper looper tension is too loose.

The lower looper tension is too loose if it is wrapping around the edge to the top side of the fabric or extending off the edge.

To correct, turn the corresponding tension dial to the right to tighten the looper tension.

Lower looper tension is too loose.

The left needle thread tension is too tight if the outer thread is buried and pulling the lower looper thread into the fabric.

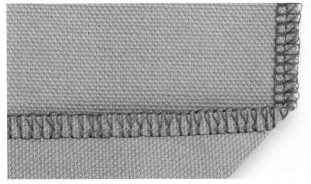

Left needle tension is too tight.

The right needle tension is too tight if the inner thread is buried and pulling the lower looper thread into the fabric.

To correct, turn the corresponding tension dial to the left to loosen the needle tension.

Right needle tension is too tight.

The left needle thread tension is too loose if the outer thread is lying on top of the fabric and leaving loops on the underside.

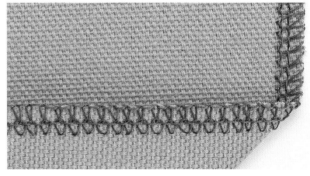

Left needle tension is too loose.

The right needle tension is too loose if the inner thread is lying on top of the fabric and leaving loops on the underside.

To correct, turn the corresponding tension dial to the right to tighten the needle tension.

Right needle tension is too loose.

Adjusting Tension on Rolled Edge

For a rolled edge, the upper looper thread should roll the edge evenly to the underside of the fabric. If the upper looper tension is too tight or the lower looper tension is too tight, the stitches will sit on the fabric surface without wrapping the edge. If the needle tension is too loose, the needle thread will form loops on the underside and the edge won't roll. Follow tension adjustments for the overlock to correct.

Tips for Success

Always check for proper threading before adjusting the tension.

Tension is affected by fabric weight and thread weight. Have scraps of the same fabric available and always test the stitch on it before beginning a project. Once you have perfected the stitch, you can begin your project with confidence!

Stitch Primer

The stitches you can make with your serger depend on the number of threads it is capable of using at once. Refer to your machine owner's manual to set up the following stitches. Always remember to test your stitches on fabric that is similar to the fabric you're using. Do this to perfect your stitch before beginning your project.

2- & 3-thread overlock

Two-thread stitches are formed with one needle and one looper. Because the stitches are less bulky, they are ideal for lightweight knits and woven fabrics. They also have more stretch than stitches formed with three or more threads. Some serger models have a 2-thread converter for the upper looper that you will need to use; check your owner's manual and follow the directions for applying the converter and for any other instructions specific to your machine for 2-thread stitching. Three-thread stitches are the most commonly used and are suitable for a wide range of fabrics and applications.

2-thread overlock

Sometimes called an overedge stitch, the threads of this stitch overlock at the edge of the fabric only and do not form a seam.

2-thread wide overlock

2-thread narrow overlock

Use this stitch for overcasting edges on lightweight or sheer fabrics, especially when using heavier threads. You also can use it for overcasting a single layer of medium-weight fabric.

3-thread overlock

This is the most popular stitch on the serger. Made with both loopers and one needle, the stitch can be wide or narrow depending on the needle position. A wide 3-thread stitch is made with the needle in the left position. A narrow 3-thread stitch is made with the needle in the right position.

3-thread narrow overlock

3-thread wide overlock

Use a wide stitch for constructing seams or finishing edges on medium- to heavy-weight knit and woven fabrics. Use a narrow stitch for constructing seams or finishing edges on lighter fabric weights and in areas that will not receive much stress. Because the stitch is stretchable, it is especially useful for knit fabrics. For a decorative edge or seam finish, use decorative threads in one or both loopers and matching serger thread in the needle. Remember to test your stitch; you will probably want to lower your tension where you are using the decorative threads.

Chain stitch

This stitch is frequently used for seams on ready-to-wear items. It is made using one needle and one looper. It is part of the 4- or 5-thread safety stitch, but it can be used alone for seams and decorative stitching. Depending on your machine, there may be a special looper or needle, or it may be part of

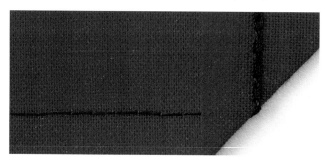

the overlock system. The chain stitch is created by stitching with the wrong side of the fabric up. This creates the chain on the right side of the fabric and a straight stitch on the wrong side. A chain stitch is very easy to pull out by pulling the looper thread to unravel the seam.

Use this stitch to make a strong seam, for decorative topstitching on the fabric surface, for quilting, or without fabric to make belt loops, tassels or trim. It is also a very fast and functional stitch for alterations and basting because it provides a strong seam and yet is very fast and easy to remove!

2- or 3-thread flat lock & ladder stitch

Simple tension adjustments to a 2- or 3-thread overlock will give you a beautiful, decorative flat lock. It is made by using one needle and the upper looper for a 2-thread flat lock, or one needle and both loopers for a 3-thread flat lock. The needle tension is loosened so the needle thread is pulled across the underside of the fabric to the outside edge. The stitch can be made wide or narrow.

3-thread wide flat lock

3-thread narrow flat lock

The ladder stitch is the reverse side of the flat lock. This stitch also is used for fagoting, a technique that catches only the edges of two pieces of fabric, leaving an open space between them. Use flat lock/ladder stitching for seaming, topstitching, hems, fagoting, couching, shirring, heirloom sewing such as joining lace with ribbon, and for other decorative effects. Because the seam allowances are eliminated, flat-lock seams are a good choice for fleece and other bulky fabrics. Decorative threads and yarns are ideal to use with decorative flat lock.

2- or 3-thread rolled edge

The rolled edge is a simple decorative stitch used to finish fabric edges. For a 2-thread rolled edge, use the right needle and lower looper. Use the right needle and both loopers for a 3-thread rolled edge. The tension for the lower looper thread is tightened to pull the needle or upper looper thread tightly around the edge of the fabric, causing it to roll. Typically, the rolled edge uses a narrow stitch finger on the throat plate.

2-thread rolled edgestitch

3-thread rolled edgestitch

Use this stitch on lightweight fabrics to edge napkins, ruffles, silky scarves or sheer window treatments. It also makes a wavy lettuce edge on knits when lightly pulled. You can stitch the rolled edge over medium-weight fishing line, narrow cord or wire for decorative edges with body and shape.

4- & 5-thread stitches

In general, 4- and 5-thread stitches have added durability and offer additional decorative options. They are the stitches most often seen on ready-to-wear items and commercial home decor accessories. Check your manual to see if your machine has these stitch capabilities.

4-thread overlock

This stitch is made with both loopers and two needles. The looper threads interlock with both needle threads to create a seam that is especially strong, but still stretches. It is more durable than a 3-thread stitch and offers an extra measure of security for seams in areas that will receive stress. For extra durability on weight-bearing seams, stitch over twill tape.

4- or 5-thread safety stitch

This stitch combines a chain stitch seam with a 2- or 3-thread overlock edge finish. It is used to make very secure seams on medium- to heavy-weight woven and knit fabrics, or for finishing edges. The stitch can be wide or narrow.

4-thread wide safety stitch

5-thread safety stitch

Use these stitches for seams that will receive a lot of wear or stress, and need to be especially sturdy.

Cover stitch

This stitch has the most stretch of any serger stitch. Often seen on ready-to-wear clothing, especially for knitwear hems, the cover stitch is a relatively new stitch on sergers. It looks like two or three parallel rows of topstitching on the right side of the fabric and decorative stitching on the wrong side. It's made by using two or three needles and one looper. The cutting system is disengaged for the cover stitch. Some machines have special plates, needle positions or looper for the cover stitch.

Use the cover stitch for hemming knits and for attaching ribbing or elastic. It can also be used with decorative threads for embellishments, and either side of the stitch can be used on the right side of the fabric. The underside of the stitch can be used to make cover-stitch lace. ❖

Triple cover stitch

Wide cover stitch

Narrow cover stitch

Chapter Two: Supplies

Needles, thread, specialty feet and sewing notions … once you have the right supplies your serger will take you places you could only dream of going with a regular sewing machine. In this section, we'll help you decide the best products to use with your fabric and project. Get ready for professional-looking results and endless creative options!

Needles

Most sergers use conventional sewing machine needles but be sure to check your owner's manual because some do require that you use special serger needles. Selecting the right needle for the fabric, thread and stitch type can prevent all kinds of frustration—broken needles, broken thread, holes or snags in fabric, puckered seams, uneven stitches and more. Luckily, your choices are many. Be sure to use the one that best suits your fabric and thread to ensure success.

To make the best needle selection you will need to understand the parts of a needle.

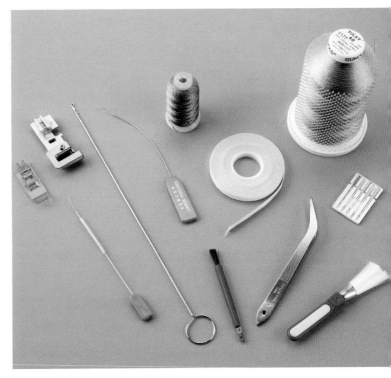

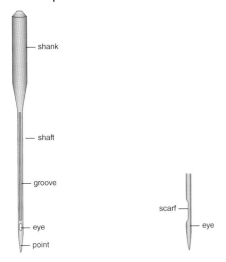

Figure 2.1   **Figure 2.2**

Shank: The top part of the needle that is inserted into the sewing machine.

Shaft: The remainder of the needle below the shank. The diameter of the shaft determines the needle size and includes the following parts:

Groove: The slit on the front of the needle above the eye. The groove protects the thread as the needle stitches through the fabric.

Scarf: The indentation on the back of the needle. It allows the bobbin thread to pass closely to the eye of the needle. A long scarf enables the bobbin hook to loop the thread easily and helps avoid skipped stitches.

Eye: The hole in the lower part of the shaft. The size increases with needle size. The eye size should be large enough to allow the thread to pass though easily.

Point: The tip of the needle that penetrates the fabric and carries the thread past the bobbin to form the stitch. The length and sharpness of the point varies among different types of needles.

Needle Types
Photos courtesy of Schmetz Needles

Universal Needle

Sizes/Features: 60/8 to 120/19. Slightly rounded point is rounded enough for stitching knits, yet pointed enough for stitching woven fabrics.

Use/Fabrics: General stitching on woven and knit fabrics in a wide range of weights.

Ball Point Needle

Sizes/Features: 70/10 to 100/16. Point is more rounded than Universal point.

Use/Fabrics: Needle slides between yarns of knits instead of piercing them, eliminating risk of snags or holes. Good for spandex and interlock knits that run easily; also good for creating even stitches on heavy knits.

Sharp/Microtex Needle

Sizes/Features: 60/8 to 110/18. Sharp point and narrow shaft.

Use/Fabrics: Ideal for very straight stitching, topstitching, heirloom sewing and pintucks. Use on smooth, finely woven fabrics like microfibers, silk, chintz and lightweight faux suede. Also good for precise stitching on appliqués.

Denim/Jeans Needle

Sizes/Features: 70/10 to 110/18. Stiff, thick, strong shank that resists breaking; also has a very sharp point.

Use/Fabrics: Use for stitching multiple layers of fabric and tightly woven fabrics like denim, canvas and cotton duck.

Machine Embroidery Needle

Sizes/Features: 75/10 to 90/14. Large eye and special scarf designed to protect thread while stitching dense designs at high speeds. It will also prevent thread from shredding and breaking.

Use/Fabrics: Machine embroidering with rayon and many other specialty threads. Use on any fabric.

Metallic Needle

Sizes/Features: 80/12 to 90/14. Larger eye than machine embroidery enables stitching with heavier threads. Large groove and specially designed scarf protect delicate threads and prevent shredding during stitching.

Use/Fabrics: Designed for use with metallic thread on any fabric.

Quilting Needle

Sizes/Features: 75/11 and 90/14. Sharp, tapered point.

Use/Fabrics: Designed for stitching through multiple fabric layers and intersecting seams. Use for piecing quilts and quilting layers together.

Stretch Needle

Sizes/Features: 65/9 to 90/14. Deep scarf allows bobbin hook to get closer to the needle eye and prevents skipped stitches on fine, lightweight knit fabrics.

Use/Fabrics: Use for swimwear, fabrics containing spandex, synthetic suedes, silk jersey and other elasticized lightweight knits.

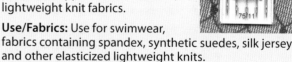

Topstitch Needle

Sizes/Features: 80/12, 90/14 and 100/16. Extra-sharp point. Extra-large eye and large groove accommodate topstitching and other heavyweight threads.

Use/Fabrics: Use for straight, accurate stitching with heavier threads on a variety of fabrics. Can also be used for machine embroidery when using heavy threads.

Threads

One of the advantages of a serger is that you can use a wide variety of threads—heavyweights, decorative and even special serger yarns in the loopers. This lets you embellish surfaces and edges in ways you can't duplicate with a standard sewing machine.

Selecting Threads

Quality counts when it comes to choosing threads for your serger project. Inexpensive threads may appear to be a bargain, but don't be fooled! They fray, break, create skipped stitches and produce excess lint in your machine. High-quality threads will result in smooth, uniform stitches, fewer broken threads and a more attractive finished edge.

Remember that the needles will be stitching the seam and the loopers will be overcasting the edge. If you want to use heavier-weight decorative threads, you should use them in the loopers only and regular serger thread in the needles.

For serging seams, it usually isn't necessary to purchase three or four cones of each color for a project. Instead, match the needle thread to the fabric and finish the edges with a complementary color or a neutral color such as taupe or gray. You may want all threads to match for rolled edges, flat lock or chain stitching. Experiment with using various types of decorative threads in interesting combinations to find the ones you like the best.

For best results, use thread that is cross-wound on a cone. These threads unwind from the top without spinning, making them the best choice for feeding smoothly through the machine and for the serger's high speed. In addition to threads labeled as serger, some cotton, rayon, metallic, nylon, polyester and other decorative threads are also available on cones.

And you don't always have to use threads on cones. Most sergers come with thread adapters—or these may be purchased—that allow you to use a variety of spool types and even bobbins on your serger.

Thread Types

All of the following threads are intended for use in sergers, although some heavier threads are only suitable in the loopers and not for use in the needles. For best results, always test thread with the stitch and fabric similar to that which you will be using.

Tip for Success

Sew slowly when using decorative threads.

Begin a test sample with at least a 3.5mm stitch length to keep the fabric moving under the foot.

Serger thread

Thread labeled as serger thread is intended for use in the needles or the loopers for general-purpose serging. These threads are finer than all-purpose sewing threads, making them more suitable for serging by reducing bulk and resulting in smooth, supple stitching.

Usually this thread is made with core-spun polyester. Good-quality threads are smooth, uniform and strong—important attributes for passing through the thread guides, tension discs and loopers at high speeds. And they are suitable for use on most fabrics.

Woolly nylon thread

This soft thread has little or no twist, and it spreads out to provide excellent coverage. It produces a soft, stretchy seam.

It is available in solid, variegated and metallic colors in two weights. The color is heat set, making it durable and permanent. The heavier weight provides extra coverage.

It is ideal for rolled edges, knits and lingerie.

It is recommended for use in the loopers, but can be used in the needle. Use a dental-floss threader or double-eye needle threader to help insert this untwisted thread through the needle or looper eyes.

Because nylon melts, use a press cloth when pressing and use on projects that will be air-dried or dried on low heat when laundered.

For best results, loosen tension, shorten stitch length and widen the stitch width.

Rolled edge with woolly nylon

Tip for Success

Use a press cloth to avoid touching a hot iron directly to decorative threads, especially those made of nylon and metallic fibers. These threads may melt or flatten with direct heat.

Metallic thread

These threads are made with metallic foil twisted with polyester or nylon, and have little or no stretch. They are available in machine embroidery weights and heavier weights. Heavier weights provide good edge coverage.

Use this thread for decorative stitching and edge finishes that don't need to stretch. Also, it can be used for rolled edges in the upper looper only.

Use a metallic needle and loosen the tension slightly.

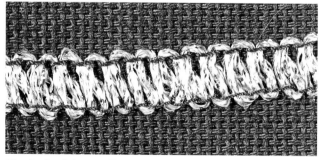

Flat lock with metallic thread

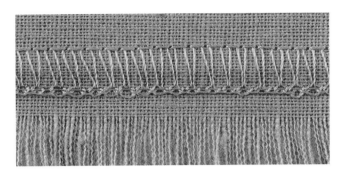

Rayon thread

Rayon thread

Rayon threads feature beautiful colors with a high luster available in 30 wt. and 40 wt. machine embroidery threads and heavier weight decorative threads.

Rayon isn't as strong as polyester or acrylic thread, and should not be used for seams. Consider using a stronger thread for the needle(s) and rayon thread in the loopers.

Use embroidery threads for heirloom serging, flat locking and rolled edges.

Use heavier weights of rayon in the loopers only for decorative stitching, including edge finishes, flat locking and rolled edges. Loosen the tension and widen the stitch for edge finishes and flat locking. Use in the upper looper only for rolled edges.

Polyester thread & floss

These soft, smooth threads are colorfast, resistant to bleach, strong and durable.

Use thread in needles and loopers. Use floss in the loopers or in a size 90 needle.

Ideal for projects for babies and children.

Use in upper looper only for rolled edges.

Polyester floss

Cotton thread

Cotton threads are soft, durable, have a matte finish and are available in a wide range of solid and blended colors.

Use heavier 12 wt. cotton threads in the loopers to create a full, thick edge finish or decorative seam. Use 30 wt. cotton threads in the needles and loopers.

Good for construction and decorative stitching.

Best for use on natural, woven fabrics.

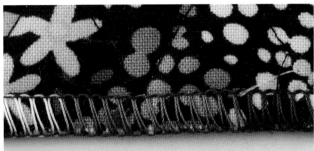

Overlock with cotton thread

Pearl cotton embroidery thread

Mercerized cotton threads are soft, shiny and loosely twisted.

Use in the upper looper only. For best results, use a wide stitch, loosen the tension slightly and lengthen the stitch length.

Nice for finishing edges, flat locking and as filler for overlock or rolled edges.

Flat lock with pearl cotton

Serger yarn

Designed specifically for serging, this yarn is a fine, acrylic fiber that adds softness and texture to edges and decorative stitches. Other very fine yarns can be used as serging yarn substitutes.

Use in the upper looper for a flat lock or for a heavier rolled edge.

Use in both loopers for an overlock.

Ideal for finishing edges on fleece, blankets and sweater knits.

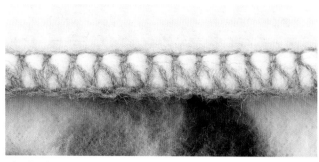

Flat lock with serger yarn

Accessories & Notions

Just like your sewing machine, your serger has special accessories to expand your creative options and helpful notions designed to make your life easier. The following are just a few of the many available. Check with your machine dealer or manufacturer's website for more accessories and notions.

Basting tape

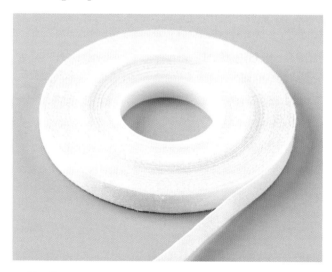

Self-adhesive, double-sided basting tape is perfect for holding edges together. This is a good substitute for pinning too close to the edge and taking a chance of nicking the blades on a pin.

Dental Floss Threaders

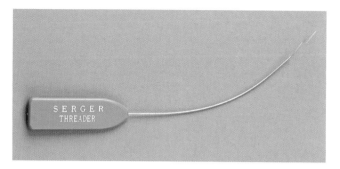

This inexpensive threader makes it easy to thread the loopers, especially when you are using fuzzy threads like wooly nylon or heavy threads like serger yarns.

Lint brush

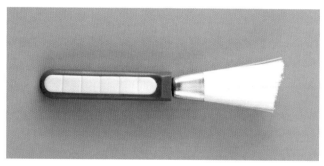

Use this brush to keep the loopers and blades free of excess lint.

Loop turner

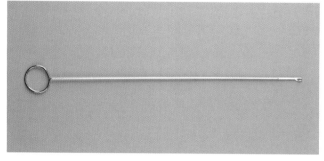

This is great for pulling serger tails under the stitching at the ends of your stitching to secure the threads.

Needle inserter

A needle inserter holds the needle to make it easy to insert into the machine.

Seam sealant

Ideal for securing thread ends and preventing fabric edges from fraying. Dab a bit at the end of fabric, let it dry and then cut off the rest of the thread chain.

Thread nets

Use these nets over thread cones to prevent sliding and tangling thread.

Tweezers

Serger tweezers have long serrated tips for grasping serger threads while threading your serger in those tight places.

Trim catcher

This handy waste tray hangs over the edge of your sewing table to catch the fabric and threads that are trimmed off when you're serging. Some sergers come with a trim catcher, or you can purchase one from sewing machine dealers, catalogs or online. ❖

Specialty Presser Feet

Pearl Foot: Used for attaching pearl and bead trims.

Gathering Foot: Also known as a shirring foot or separator foot, it is used for joining two pieces of fabric while gathering one of the layers as it is attached.

Elastic Foot: Guides the elastic and stretches it as you sew.

Piping Foot: Available in two sizes, one for applying standard-size piping and a larger version for decorator piping.

Clear Foot: This foot is designed for optional use with the cover stitch.

Blind Hem Foot: This foot is designed to create almost invisible hems. It has a special guide plate that rests along a fold in the fabric while stitching the hem seam, and trimming and finishing the hem edge.

Chapter Three: Stitch Techniques

Get ready to play with all the stitches your serger has waiting for you to explore! There are six basic serger stitches: overlock, flat lock, rolled edge, chain, blanket and cover stitch. In general, these each have a wide or narrow seam width, and long or short stitch length. And best of all, each stitch can be used with decorative threads.

4-Thread & 3-Thread Overlock

The 4-thread overlock is the most popular stitch on a serger. It is created by using both needles

Tip for Success

To reinforce seams that will receive a lot of stress, use a 4- or 5-thread safety stitch. A safety stitch is the fourth thread in a 4-thread stitch or the chain stitch in a 5-thread stitch. Or stitch over twill tape or ribbon placed on the seam line with a 4-thread overlock.

and both loopers. Because it produces a strong seam with two lines of needle stitches, it is ideal for construction of garments and home decor projects. It also provides an attractive and sturdy edge finish. Use it on fabrics ranging from denim to lightweight cottons and knits. Generally, the left needle in a 4-thread stitch is ¼ inch from the cutting blade—be sure to calculate this when planning your seam allowance and how much fabric to trim as you serge.

Because it only uses one needle and both loopers, the 3-thread overlock has more stretch and is lighter weight than a 4-thread overlock. It is ideal for edge finishing and for seams that don't need the reinforcement of a second line of needle stitches. You can stitch a wide 3-thread stitch by using the left needle or a narrow 3-thread stitch by using the right needle.

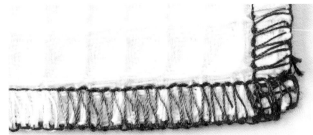

3-thread wide overlock

Tip for Success

Test the stitch with the thread and fabric you'll be using before beginning your project. This will enable you to adjust stitch width and length, tension and the differential feed as needed to successfully serge the project fabric right the first time. A perfect seam should have balanced tension, not pucker or stretch the fabric, and stay securely stitched when you pull on both layers of the fabric.

Stitching a Seam

Before you begin serging a seam, make a test sample using scraps of the same fabric to ensure that the stitch width and tension settings are correct.

For most fabrics, pins aren't necessary because the serger feeds evenly. If you do need to use them, pin away from the seam line and be sure to remove them before they reach the blades. Running over a pin with your blade can seriously damage it—and replacing blades can get expensive! You can also use self-adhesive, double-sided basting tape to hold the layers together.

Begin stitching by inserting the fabric under the toe of the foot, and the feed dogs will grab it and pull it under.

Tip for Success

You may need to lift the presser foot for heavy-weight or slippery fabrics. Holding the fabric lightly as you begin stitching, use your hands to guide the fabric and control how much is being cut off. Serge at a medium or high speed when seaming heavy-weight fabrics—a slow speed will also slow down the cutting blade and may result in uneven trimming.

Securing Thread Chain Tails at the Ends of a Seam

It's important to secure thread tails at the end of seams to prevent raveling. There are several ways to do this.

Use seam sealant

Knot the chain at the end of the seam. Apply a drop of seam sealant to the knot (Figure 3.1) and let it dry. Cut the excess thread chain. ***Note:*** *Excess seam sealant can be removed with rubbing alcohol.*

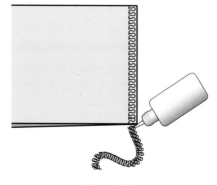

Figure 3.1

Bury the thread chain

Insert the thread chain through the eye of a tapestry needle (Figure 3.2a) and slide under the looper threads. Trim the excess chain. Insert a bodkin or loop turner through the looper threads and grasp the thread chain (Figure 3.2b). Pull the chain back through the looper threads and trim the excess chain (Figure 3.2c).

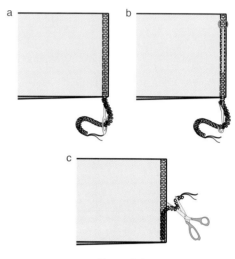

Figure 3.2

Use the serger

To secure the chain at the beginning of a seam, stitch one stitch into the edge of the fabric (Figure 3.3a), then lift the presser foot. Bring the chain to the front of the needle. Pull on the chain to tighten it and place it on the seam allowance (Figure 3.3b). Continue serging, stitching over the chain (Figure 3.3c).

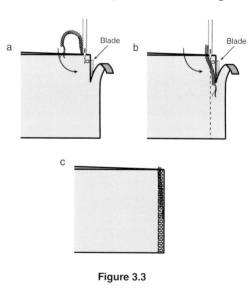

Figure 3.3

To secure the chain at the end of a seam, serge one stitch off the edge of the fabric and slide the fabric off the stitch finger (Figure 3.4a). Raise the presser foot and pull a small amount of slack in the needle thread. Pull on the thread to tighten it, and then turn the fabric over and place the chain on the serged edge. Stitch over the edge again for one or two inches (Figure 3.4b), being careful not to cut the stitches already on the fabric. Trim the excess chain.

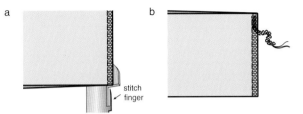

Figure 3.4

Turning Outside Corners

The cutting system on your serger trims the fabric before it is sewn. Serging shapes will take practice, and it may take a while before you feel comfortable following these techniques.

1. Serge one stitch past the corner and stop.

2. Raise the presser foot and raise the needle out of the fabric.

3. Pull a little slack in the needle thread and slip the fabric off the stitch finger. *Note: Too much slack in the thread will leave a loop on the corner.* Turn the fabric to stitch the next edge. Lower the presser foot and pull on the needle thread slightly to tighten it.

4. Continue serging.

Turning Inside Corners

Serging an inside corner is easier to do than an outside corner and is like serging a straight line. Stay-stitch 1-inch on both sides of corner along the seamline and again ⅛-inch from the edge to stabilize fabric. Clip corner just to first stay-stitching. Serge one edge until the knife reaches the corner (Figure 3.5a) and then straighten the edge and continue stitching (Figure 3.5b).

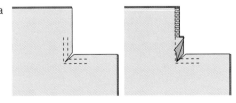

Figure 3.5

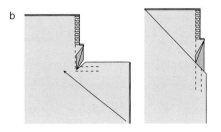

Figure 3.5

Curves

Inside curves, such as necklines, are simple to sew. Gently pull on the fabric to make it straight as you serge (Figure 3.6a).

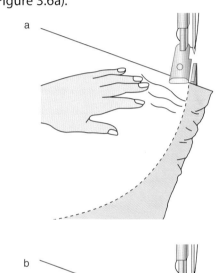

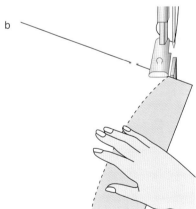

Figure 3.6

Outside curves require a little more fabric handling. For an outside curve, use your fingertips to continually push the fabric against the cutting system (Figure 3.6b). Because of the feed dogs' ability to grab and evenly feed the fabric, the outside curve will turn out nicely with this technique.

Seam Allowance Finishes

In addition to stitching seams on the serger, you can give traditional seams stitched on a sewing machine a professional look when you finish the seam allowances with overcast that prevents raveling. Use a 3- or 4-thread overlock for medium- to heavy-weight fabrics and a 2-thread overlock for lightweight fabrics, heavier threads or to reduce bulk.

Serger welt seam

This seam works well with heavier fabrics like fleece or wool where you don't want the seam exposed and want to eliminate bulk. It is a combination of a straight stitch with your sewing machine and an overlock serger stitch.

1. With wrong sides together, straight stitch the seam.

2. Trim one seam allowance to ¼ inch.

3. Finish the remaining seam allowance with a 3- or 4-thread overlock without trimming.

4. Press the seam open; then press the serged seam over the trimmed seam.

5. Topstitch into place (Figure 3.7).

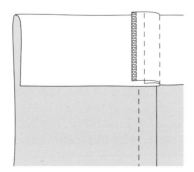

Figure 3.7

French serger seam

This seam finish encloses the raw edges of the fabric, making it a perfect seam finish for sheer fabrics that fray. This seam works well for side seams, sheer draperies and when you don't want the serging to show.

1. Set your serger to a mid-width 3-thread overlock.

2. With wrong sides together, serge and trim seam allowance.

3. Press the serged seam flat to set the stitches.

4. Open the seam and press the serging to one side.

5. Fold the fabric right sides together and straight stitch with your sewing machine just past the serged seam encased in the fabric (Figure 3.8).

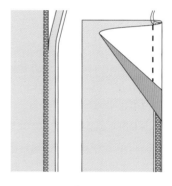

Figure 3.8

Blind Hem

A blind hem is an ideal finish for heavier fabrics such as fleece, wool, denim and draperies. Use the blind hem technique when you don't want the hem stitches to show. Be sure to test this stitch on a scrap of the same or similar fabric to perfect your technique and ensure you have it set up to be secure and yet "invisible." Here's how:

1. Set your serger for a 3- or 4-thread overlock.

2. Lengthen and widen the stitch.

3. Determine the hem allowance.

4. Lightly press the hem up to the wrong side.

5. Fold the fabric back on itself, leaving at least ¼ inch of the hem extending beyond the fold.

6. Place the fold of the hem under the foot and begin sewing, barely catching the folded fabric edge with the needle and trimming the extending hem (Figure 3.9).

Figure 3.9

7. Use the adjustable guide to the right of the foot to determine the "bite" of the stitch. If too much thread shows on the right side, move the guide farther away from the needle (to the right). Move it to the left if the needle isn't catching enough fabric to secure the hem.

Flat Lock or Ladder Stitch

A flat lock seam is formed with one needle, usually the left, with very loose tension and the lower looper only. The stitches form loops that extend past the edge being serged and lie flat on the surface of the fabric or between two joined panels when pulled. The distance the loops extend determines how flat the stitches will lie or if there will be space between two adjoining fabric panels. Use it as a functional, stretchy seam for knitwear and a surface embellishment on both the flat lock and ladder stitch seam sides.

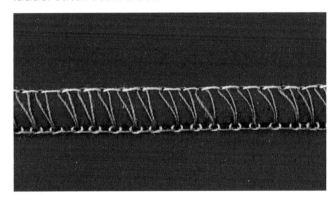

Stitch Setup

Use two or three threads for flat lock. Two-thread stitches are easier to open and flatten, while 3-thread stitches are more durable for seams.

2-thread setup

1. A 2-thread wide overlock may require a 2-thread converter (a spring that closes the eye of the upper looper). Check your manual for specifics.

2. Use the left needle and lower looper.

3. Begin with a balanced setting and then loosen the needle tension so the thread loops form slightly beyond the cut edge to achieve a flat seam when stitches are pulled.

3-thread setup

1. Use a flat lock setting on computerized machines or 3-thread wide overlock.

2. Use the left needle and both loopers.

3. Loosen the needle thread tension and tighten the lower looper tension.

4. Loosen the upper looper tension *only* if needed—test first. The thread loops should form slightly beyond the cut edge in order for the stitches to lie flat when pulled.

Tips for Success

For flat lock seams on fabrics that ravel, finish the edges with narrow overlock and then press the seam allowance under. Stitch the folded edges together with a flat lock.

For flat lock seams on fabrics like fleece, felted wool or other thick, non-fraying fabrics, cut off the seam allowances before stitching the edges together.

Stitching the Seams

When flat lock seams are stitched correctly, the raw or folded edges should butt together when opened flat. Serge the seam with wrong sides together to see the flat lock loops on the right side of the fabric. If you want to see the ladder stitch on the right side of the fabric, serge the seam with right sides together.

1. Position the fabric edges under the foot so the stitches will extend halfway off the fabric as you stitch. Extend the loops past the fabric edges more for heavier fabrics and less for lighter weights (Figure 3.10).

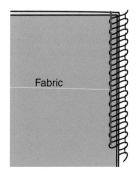

Fabric

Figure 3.10

2. Guide the fabric evenly as you stitch to ensure a straight edge.

3. Pull gently on the two layers of fabric until the stitches lie flat.

4. For seams that will receive stress, press a ⅝-inch-wide strip of fusible tricot over the stitches on the wrong side of the seam (Figure 3.11).

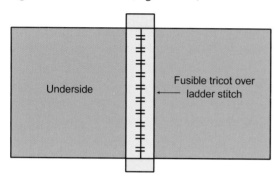

Figure 3.11

Flat Lock Hem

Use this hemming technique to add decorative stitching along the hem. Finish the hem edge with overlock. Determine your hem allowance and set your serger for flat lock.

For flat lock on the right side:

1. Press the hem allowance to the wrong side twice and press lightly.

2. Stitch a flat lock next to the fold as shown, being careful not to cut the fabric (Figure 3.12).

3. Pull the hem down and press.

Figure 3.12

For ladder stitches on the right side:

1. Press the hem allowance to the wrong side (Figure 3.13a).

2. Fold the hem up to the right side with ¼ inch of the hem allowance edge extending beyond the fold.

3. Stitch a flat lock to overlap the fold and hem edge; trim off the ¼-inch hem allowance (Figure 3.13b).

4. Pull the hem down and press (Figure 3.13c).

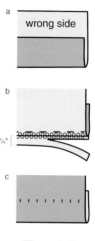

Figure 3.13

Decorative Flat Lock

Flat lock along folds to create decorative accents on the surface of the fabric using either the flat-lock loops or ladder stitch on the right side. Stitch using the techniques given for seams.

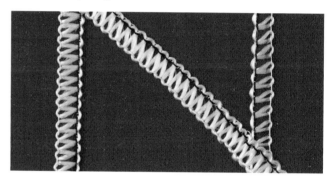

Decorative Ladder Stitch

Fold fabric right sides together and flat lock along the fold. Open fold and flatten. Thread a tapestry needle, or double-eyed needle, with ribbon floss, narrow ribbon or any narrow decorative trim. Weave needle in and out of the ladder stitches.

Flat Lock Fringe

Here's a quick and easy way to fringe the edges of an evenly woven fabric to make place mats, table runners, scarves and more.

1. Cut the fabric on the straight grain for even fringing.

2. Use a water- or air-soluble marker to mark the stitching line.

3. Fold the fabric on the marked line and flat lock along the fold.

4. Bury the end of the thread chain under the stitches on the wrong side, and then pull the seam flat.

5. Starting at the raw edge of the fabric, remove the horizontal threads up to the stitching.

Fagoting

A beautiful heirloom stitching technique, fagoting is achieved by using the ladder stitch side of the flat lock to fill a space between two pieces of fabric. A 2-thread flat lock is stronger than a 3-thread because the 2-thread interlocks at each stitch.

1. Use a wide 2-thread flat lock and thread the needle and looper with the same decorative thread, or thread the needle with decorative thread and the looper with monofilament thread.

2. Fold each piece of fabric wrong sides together where flat lock will be stitched.

3. Align the folds with right sides together and stitch, just catching the edges of the folds in the stitching and having the loops hang halfway over the edges (Figure 3.14a).

4. Gently pull the pieces apart to flatten the stitches. There should be an even space between the fabric pieces connected by the ladders of the flat lock (Figure 3.14b).

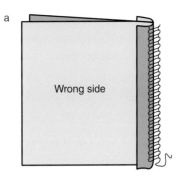

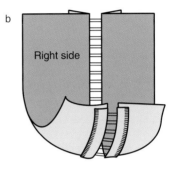

Figure 3.14

Blanket Stitch

The blanket stitch is perfect for finishing the edges of heavy-weight fabrics such as fleece, wool and denim. The left needle thread wraps to the edge on both sides of the fabric and the looper threads meet along the edge of the fabric.

1. Set up your machine for a 2-thread flat lock.

2. Use heavy-weight or decorative thread in the needle and regular serger thread in the looper.

3. Lengthen and widen the stitch as much as possible.

4. Loosen the needle tension all the way—you may need to remove it from the tension disc and guide.

5. Tighten the tension on both loopers all the way.

6. Disengage the blade if possible.

7. Hold the fabric taut and stitch along the edge.

Note: Do not cut the fabric with the blades if they cannot be disengaged. If necessary, use tweezers to pull the stitches to the edge as needed.

Tip for Success

To make sure the stitches lie along the fabric edge, wrap water-soluble stabilizer around the edge before stitching the blanket stitch. Then pull the stitches to the edges and remove the stabilizer.

Rolled Edge

You can use two or three threads for rolled edges. Use a 2-thread rolled edge on very lightweight fabrics such as silks and sheers, or a 3-thread rolled edge on other soft lightweight fabrics. The rolled edge technique cuts, folds and overlocks the edge. Most machines have a rolled-edge setting; refer to your owner's manual for stitch setup.

Tips for Success

When serging a 3-thread rolled edge and the upper looper thread doesn't meet the needle thread on the underside of the fabric, slightly tighten the lower looper tension. If there are loops on the top or edge of the fabric, slightly tighten the upper looper.

Lengthen the stitch length to create a picot edge.

Wrap lightweight water-soluble stabilizer around the fabric edge before stitching to prevent threads from poking through.

Rolled edge over wire or fishing line

Use a 3-thread rolled edge to create shapable rolled edges. A wired edge is perfect for adding a fun touch to ruffled edges and other lightweight edges, or for creating your own wire-edge ribbons. An edge rolled over fishing line gives body to the edge of sheer or lightweight drapery panels or table covers. You also can use pearl cotton or lightweight cord instead of wire or fishing line.

These stitches are easily completed when you use a cording foot to feed the wire or fishing line through as you stitch. Or you can carefully feed the wire or fishing line under the stitches as you go.

Rolled edge over wire

Rolled edge over fishing line

Lettuce rolled edge

Create this edge on knit fabrics by stretching and holding the fabric tight as you stitch. Do not pull the fabric—you will damage your serger!

Note: Practice on scraps on the same grainline as your project. Be aware that some fabrics do not lettuce well.

Woolly nylon threads work especially well for this stitch because of their stretchy quality.

If more stretch is desired, try increasing the presser foot pressure.

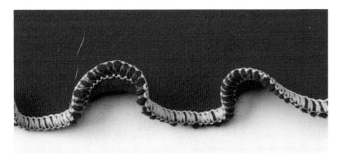

Chain Stitch

Machine capabilities and setup for the chain stitch vary, so consult your manual. On most machines you set up the chain stitch by using the left or front needle, chain stitch looper, disengaging the upper blade and possibly changing the presser foot and needle plate.

Seaming & basting

A chain stitch is ideal for seaming and provides a strong, durable stitch. Be sure to secure the seam ends since this seam is easily pulled out. For this same reason, chain stitching is ideal for basting. When chain stitch seaming, be sure to stitch with the wrong side of the fabric up.

Decorative chain stitching

For decorative stitches, stitch on the right side of the fabric using medium- to heavy-weight thread in the chain-stitch looper and regular serger thread in the needle. Use the chain stitch to:

• Quilt layers together on small quilts.

• Create decorative rows of stitching or edge stitching on pillows, linens and other projects.

• Sew a hand-quilted look, using a monofilament thread in the chain-stitch looper.

• Sew heirloom stitching with rayon thread to create mock pintucks or to decorate the center of a length of ribbon.

Cover Stitch

Machine capabilities and setup for the cover stitch vary. Consult your owner's manual. The cover stitch is made with two or three needles, and looks similar to the chain stitch. It creates decorative stitching on the underside of the fabric and a straight stitch on top. Either side of the stitch can be used on the right side of the fabric.

Hems

The 6mm-wide cover stitch is the garment industry standard for hemming. A very elastic stitch, it is especially suitable for knits and for hemming home decor projects.

Decorative stitching

For decorative stitches, use the loop side of the stitch on the right side of the fabric and place decorative thread in the looper. Use the cover stitch to:

• Create parallel rows of decorative stitching with wide, narrow or triple cover stitches.

• Attach flat lace and trims. Use a wide cover stitch, stitching close to the edge of the lace to prevent the edge from curling. Use a matching-width cover stitch to topstitch ribbon and braided trim (Figure 3.15).

Figure 3.15

Mock flat felled

Easily create the look of flat felled seams on heavy-weight fabrics such as denim or fleece by serging the fabrics together with right sides facing using a 4- or 5-thread overlock. Press the serged edge to one side and stitch in place from the right side using a cover stitch (Figure 3.16).

Figure 3.16

Fagoting

Create fagoting between fabric panels and/or ribbon strips with a wide cover stitch. Spray the wrong side of two fabrics and/or ribbon strips with temporary spray adhesive following the manufacturer's instructions.

Position pieces right side up and spaced ¼ inch apart on a piece of water-soluble stabilizer. Serge a wide cover stitch down the center of the ¼-inch space, catching either side of the fabric/ribbon edges in the stitching (Figure 3.17).

Remove the water-soluble stabilizer following manufacturer's instructions. ❖

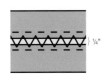

Figure 3.17

Chapter Four: Creative Options

There is so much more you can do with your serger than simply stitch seams and finish edges. The following techniques save time and expand creative serging options.

Applying Binding

It's quick and easy to apply binding to a quilt when you use a serger.

1. With right side of binding facing the quilt top, use a 3- or 4-thread overlock to serge bias binding around the edges of the layered quilt. *Note: This will compact the layers making it easy to wrap the binding to the back.*

2. Fold the binding to the quilt back and hand-stitch the binding edge in place, or machine-stitch in the ditch using a sewing machine from the front to secure the edge.

Gathering & Ruffles

Gathering is frequently a time-consuming task. Using the following serger techniques to make gathered edges and ruffles will save you time and produce even-gathered edges and ruffles for heirloom, home decorating and garment sewing.

Gathered edges with differential feed

Set the differential feed to 2-2.5 and stitch the edge using a 4-thread overlock. The adjusted differential feed system will feed more fabric into the front feed dogs as you stitch. To further increase the gathering, leave 12-inch-long thread tails at each end of the stitching. Adjust the gathers by pulling the needle threads.

Tip for Success

Increasing the presser foot pressure to 5 will increase gathering, as more pressure is applied to the fabric as it moves under the foot.

Gathering with a rolled edge or flat lock

Follow the instructions for stitching a rolled edge over fishing line found in Chapter 3, page 28, sliding the fabric on the fishing line to gather (Figure 1).

Figure 1

Or stitch over cord or elastic with a flat lock, and then pull the cord or elastic to gather the fabric (Figure 4.2).

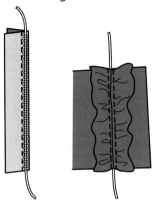

Figure 4.2

Ruffles

For easy-to-make ruffles with one gathered edge, finish one long edge with a rolled edge on lightweight fabrics or a 2- or 3-thread overcast on heavier fabrics. Use one of the gathering methods above to gather the opposite long edge.

For a ruffle that is gathered in the center, finish both long edges of the ruffle strip with a rolled edge or overcast. Fold the ruffle strip in half lengthwise with right sides together. Serge a flat lock over a cord or elastic along the fold.

Pintucks

Pintucks are best sewn on lightweight fabrics such as batiste, and are ideal for heirloom sewing projects. Check your owner's manual to see if your machine requires a pintuck or rolled-edge foot for best results.

1. Set your machine up for a 3-thread rolled edge with decorative rayon thread in the upper looper. Adjust the tension settings to 3 for the needle, 5 for the upper looper and 6 for the lower looper. Lock or disengage blades if possible.

2. Use a water-soluble marker to draw parallel pintuck lines on the fabric, spaced ½ to 1 inch apart.

3. Fold the fabric wrong sides together along each marked line and stitch along the fold, being careful not to cut the fabric if the blade cannot be disengaged. ❖

Chapter Five: Maintenance & Troubleshooting

careful to avoid blowing air into your machine, which can force the lint and trimmings deeper into the machine.

- Clean the blades with cotton swabs and a very small amount of alcohol. After they have dried, apply a small amount of oil to the blades, wiping off excess oil so it doesn't get on your fabric.

- Loosen tensions completely and floss with non-waxed dental floss or a folded, lightweight strip of fabric to remove broken threads, fibers and lint.

- Change needles often. Dull or bent needles will adversely affect your stitching and may even tear the fabric.

- Follow the manufacturer's recommendations for how often to oil your machine. Clean out all lint first; then apply oil to the suggested moving parts in the amounts recommended.

- Have your serger professionally maintained on a regular basis. Consult with your machine dealer and your owner's manual regarding this service.

- Cover the serger when not in use. Most come with a cover, but they are readily available at fabric stores and machine dealers.

Troubleshooting

Serging is fun, but when you have problems the fun turns to frustration. The first step in dealing with problems is to check that the machine is properly threaded and tensions are correctly set. Following are some common problems and possible solutions.

Problem: thread breaks

- The most common cause is improper threading. Make sure the machine is threaded correctly and no threads are crossing each other or wrapped together. Also check to see if the thread is getting caught as it leaves the cone or spool.

- Tension might be too tight. Reduce it slightly on the dial for the thread that is breaking.

- Bent or dull needles can cause the thread to break.

- Old, brittle thread and low-quality threads also break easily.

Keeping your serger in excellent running condition is easy with regular maintenance and cleaning. However, please rely on a trained sewing machine dealer for regular checkups and service.

Maintenance

Proper care and maintenance can ensure a long, happy relationship between you and your serger. Follow these tips to keep your machine in tip-top working order:

- Unplug the serger before removing lint or performing other maintenance. Remove the throat plate, presser foot and disengage the blades, if possible.

- Clean lint and trimmings out of the serger after each project. You can use a stiff bristled brush, mini-vac or canned air to remove lint, being

Problem: skipped or irregular stitches

• An improper needle type or dull needle can cause skipped stitches. Check your owner's manual to see if a certain brand or type of needle is recommended for your machine.

• If using a heavy-weight fabric, increase the stitch width and length, as well as the presser foot pressure.

• Make sure the thread is feeding from the cones or spools properly.

Problem: puckered fabric

• Adjust the differential feed, referring to your owner's manual.

• Make sure the stitch finger is in the correct position.

• Check tensions—you may need to loosen the tension on the needle or one of the loopers.

• Decrease the presser foot pressure.

• Widen the stitch width if the edge is pulling in.

Problem: stretched fabric

• Adjust the differential feed, referring to your owner's manual.

• Lighten the presser foot pressure and/or length of the stitch.

• Stabilize the fabric edge before stitching by wrapping with water-soluble stabilizer.

• Be careful not to pull the fabric as you serge.

Problem: seam stitches show

• Needle tension is too loose. Increase the tension one number at a time and test after each change.

• Thread may not be completely set in the guides. Rethread.

• Machine may have been threaded while tension was engaged. Loosen tensions and rethread.

Problem: overcast loops not aligned with or hanging off fabric edge

• Looper tensions may need adjusting.

• Thread may have slipped out of thread guide. Rethread.

• Adjust the cutting width.

Problem: rolled edge pulling away from fabric

• If the fabric is loosely woven, the rolled edge may pull away—try lengthening the stitch and using the smallest needle possible to lessen the number and size of needle holes in the edge.

• Wrap the edge with a strip of water-soluble stabilizer before stitching.

• Use your sewing machine to stitch a straight line along the fabric edge before stitching the rolled edge.

Problem: trimmed edge is ragged

• One or both of the blades may be nicked or dull and need replacing.

• If you are serging heavy fabric like fleece, it could be that you were serging too slowly. Serge at a medium to high speed to ensure even cutting.

Problem: fabric threads poke through rolled edge

• Use a thread with good coverage, such as woolly nylon.

• Wrap the edge with a strip of water-soluble stabilizer before stitching.

• Adjust the stitch so more fabric is turned under.

Problem: flat lock doesn't lie flat

• Position the fabric so the stitches are hanging farther off the fold or edge.

• A 2-thread flat lock will flatten more easily than a 3-thread stitch.

• Make sure the fabric has enough body to maintain an edge for flat locking.

Problem: machine jamming

• Be sure to insert fabric in front of the cutter and not behind it.

• Thread may be caught under the presser foot. After stitching, be sure to leave a thread tail behind the presser foot that is long enough not to pull under when you start stitching.

• Make sure the fabric that is being trimmed off isn't going into the machine under the presser foot. ❖

Party Sampler Pillow

Designer's Notes
Showcase beautiful threads when you embellish a pillow panel with decorative flat locking on folds.

Serger Skill Level
Beginner

Finished Size
18 x 18 inches

Serger Skill
Decorative flat locking on folds for embellishment

Materials
- 44/45-inch-wide 100-percent cotton fabric:
   1½ yards multicolored print fabric
- 1⅛ yards ³⁄₁₆-inch fusible piping
- ⅝ yard fusible tricot interfacing
- 18 x 18-inch pillow form
- Zipper foot for sewing machine
- Press cloth
- Basic sewing supplies and equipment

Threads
- Assorted decorative and serger threads
- All-purpose coordinating sewing thread

Serger Stitches & Settings
Note: *These are suggested serger settings. Be sure to test your stitch on a scrap of project or similar fabric to ensure stitch perfection before beginning your project.*

3-thread flat lock for decorative stitching
Stitch Length: 3.0
Left Needle Tension: 1
Right Needle: Removed
Upper Looper Tension: 3
Lower Looper Tension: 6

Optional for flat locking on fold: Foot to protect fabric from cutting blade or disengage cutting blade

Tip for Success

The needle thread easily pulls out of flat locking and can unravel your stitches. To avoid this, leave long tails at each end of the stitching.

Machine Threading
Flat locking: serger thread in needle and lower looper

Decorative thread in upper looper

3-thread wide overlock: serger thread in needle and both loopers

Cutting
From the multicolored print:
Cut two 19 x 19-inch squares for the pillow front and back.

From the remaining multicolored print:
Cut 1⅜-inch-wide bias strips to equal 1⅛ yards.

From the interfacing:
Cut one 19 x 19-inch square.

Embellishing Pillow Top
1. Use a chalk pencil to draw random lines across the right side of one pillow square, referring to the project photo.

2. Fold the fabric along one marked line and flat lock along the fold. **Note:** *Half of the loop width should extend past the fold so the stitches will lie flat when the fabric is unfolded.*

3. Unfold the fabric, pull the stitches flat and press.

4. Repeat steps 2 and 3 to stitch along all lines. Change the decorative thread used in the upper looper for each line of stitching.

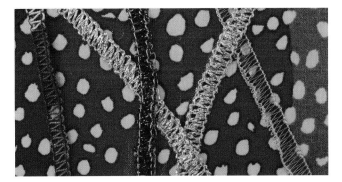

5. To add stability to the pillow top and prevent the decorative threads from pulling out, apply a 19 x 19-inch square of fusible interfacing to the wrong side of the embellished pillow top following manufacturer's instructions. Be sure to use a press cloth and lower heat when ironing over decorative threads as they can melt.

Assembly
Sew right sides together using a ¼-inch seam unless otherwise indicated.

1. Sew the bias strips together diagonally on short ends. Press seams open.

2. Wrap the wrong side of the bias strip around the fusible piping with the fabric edges even. Following manufacturer's instructions, fuse the edges together.

3. Begin in the center of one side and with raw edges even, pin the piping around the edge of the pillow back.

4. Using a sewing machine and zipper foot, begin 2 inches from one end of the piping to stitch the piping in place around the pillow back close to the cord (Figure 1). End stitching 2 inches from the seam end with needle down.

Figure 1

5. To join the piping ends, lift the zipper foot and gently pull the fabric back to expose the cord.

6. Trim the cord only, even with the piping beginning end. Trim the fabric 1 inch beyond the piping beginning (Figure 2).

Figure 2

7. Turn under the end of the fabric approximately ½ inch and wrap it around the beginning end of the piping. Lower zipper foot and continue stitching the piping in place, referring to Figure 3.

Figure 3

8. With sewing machine and zipper foot, sew the pillow top to the pillow back, stitching along the piping stitching line. Leave a 10-inch opening in the seam (Figure 4).

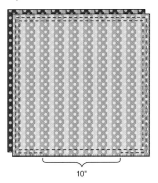

Figure 4

9. Turn the pillow panels right side out and press.

10. Insert the pillow form through the opening.

11. Turn the opening seam allowances to the inside and slipstitch closed. ❖

Credits: *Westminster Fabrics Kaffe Fassett Ombre Collection; Clover® Wrap 'n Fuse Piping; Fairfield Processing Corp. Soft Touch® pillow form; Pellon Stacy Easy Knit interfacing; threads from Sulky, YLI Corp., and Coats & Clark.*

Tip for Success
For more visual impact, shorten the stitch length when using fine metallic thread.

Piñata Panel Table Runner

Designer's Notes
It's easy to make a reversible table runner when you piece the panels together with flat locking. One side features the ladder stitch between the panels and the reverse side showcases the decorative thread used in the upper looper. Preprinted panels and a coordinating border print were used for this colorful runner with a coordinating overall print on the reverse.

Serger Skill Level
Beginner

Finished Size
19½ x 77 inches

Serger Skills
Flat lock piecing, 3-thread wide overlock

Materials
- 44/45-inch-wide 100-percent cotton fabrics:
    3 (19½-inch square) preprinted panels or
    1⅛ yards cotton print fabric *(A)*
    1⅛ yards border print fabric or ⅔ yard of coordinating print fabric *(B)*
    1⅛ yards coordinating cotton print fabric *(C)*
- 1¼ yards ball fringe with decorative header
- 1 roll ½-inch-wide fusible web
- Basic sewing supplies and equipment

Threads
- 1 cone decorative polyester floss
- 3 cones coordinating serger thread

Serger Stitches & Settings
Note: These are suggested serger settings. Be sure to test your stitch on a scrap of project or similar fabric to ensure stitch perfection before beginning your project.

3-thread wide overlock for seams and edges
Stitch Length: 2.5
Left Needle Tension: 6
Right Needle: Removed
Upper Looper Tension: 3
Lower Looper Tension: 4

3-thread flat lock for piecing
Stitch Length: 3.0
Left Needle Tension: 1
Right Needle: Removed
Upper Looper Tension: 3
Lower Looper Tension: 6

Machine Threading
Serger thread in needle and both loopers for seams

Decorative polyester floss in upper looper for flat locking and edge finish

Note: Reduce tension when using the decorative floss.

Cutting
From the preprinted panels:
Trim panels to 19½-inch squares for table runner top. *Note: If using fabric A, cut three 19½-inch squares for table runner top.*

From the border print:
Cut two 19½-inch squares with the border design centered along one edge of each square for table runner ends. *Note: If using fabric B, cut two 19½-inch squares for table runner ends.*

From the coordinating print (fabric C):
Cut three 19½-inch squares for the table runner back.

Prepare Panels
1. To assemble top panels, place a 19½-inch table runner top square right sides together with a table runner back square. Overlock together along two opposite edges using a ½-inch seam allowance. Turn right side out and press. Repeat to make 3 table runner top panels.

2. Fold each table runner end square in half wrong sides together and press. *Note: If using a border print, center the border print along one unfolded edge.*

Assembly
1. Set the serger for a flat lock with decorative polyester floss in the upper looper.

2. Place two top panels right sides together. Flat lock together, positioning the fabric edges so that slightly more than half of the stitch width extends beyond the fabric edge.

3. Pull the fabric panels until the stitches lie flat. The ladder stitch will show on the top, and the flat lock loops will show on the back. Press the stitched edges.

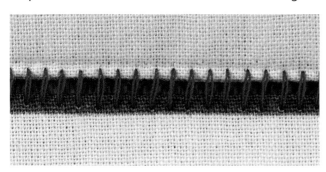

4. Repeat steps 2 and 3, attaching the remaining top panel.

5. Place an end panel on one end of the runner top with top sides together and the folded edge even with the end of the runner. Follow steps 2 and 3 to attach the end panel with flat locking.

6. Repeat to add the remaining end panel to the opposite end of the runner.

Finishing

1. Set the serger for a 3-thread wide overlock without changing the threading.

Tip for Success

Remember, the decorative thread will show on the flat-lock loop side of the stitch and not the ladder side. If you want the decorative thread and flat-lock loops to show on top of the runner, piece the panels with back sides together.

2. Overlock the edges with the decorative thread on the top of the runner.

3. Cut two 21½-inch lengths of ball fringe with the ball fringe evenly centered.

4. Turn each end of the fringe header under 1 inch. Follow manufacturer's instructions to fuse turned-under ends in place with fusible web.

5. Apply fusible web to the wrong side of header of each fringe length.

6. Remove the paper backing from fusible web. Fuse the fringe header to each end of the runner on the back side, referring to manufacturer's instructions. ❖

Credits: *Michael Miller Fabrics Gypsy Bandana collection; Expo International ball fringe; YLI Corp. Designer 7 polyester floss and Elite serger threads; The Warm Company Steam-a-Seam 2® fusible web tape.*

Strip-Pieced Fleece Throw

Designer's Notes
Make a warm and soft fleece throw even cozier when you construct and finish the edges with serger yarn. Stitching the seams with wrong sides together show-cases the yarn on the right side of the throw.

Serger Skill Level
Beginner

Finished Size
60 x 70 inches

Serger Skills
4-thread overlock seams, 4-thread overlock edge finishes, working with fleece, stitching with yarn

Materials
- 54/60-inch-wide fleece fabric:
    2 yards each of 4 coordinating fleece prints
- Basic sewing supplies and equipment

Threads
- 2 cones serger yarn
- 2 cones coordinating serger thread

Serger Stitches & Settings
Note: *These are suggested serger settings. Be sure to test your stitch on a scrap of project or similar fabric to ensure stitch perfection before beginning your project.*

4-thread overlock for seams and edges
Stitch Length: 3.0
Left Needle Tension: 6
Right Needle Tension: 3
Upper Looper Tension: 2–3
Lower Looper Tension: 2–3

Adjustments for fleece: Increase differential feed up to 2.0 as needed for seams to lie flat. Increase the stitch width to 5. ***Note:*** *Use the widest cutting/stitch width available to prevent the fleece from jamming as it is trimmed.*

Machine Threading
Serger thread in both needles

Serger yarn in both loopers

Tip for Success

When using yarn, loosen looper tensions, if needed, to achieve a balanced stitch. Stitch sample seams on project scraps to check the stitch balance.

Cutting

From each fleece print:
Cut one 8½ x 72-inch strip and one 8 x 72-inch strip.

Assembly

1. With wrong sides together and trimming ¼ inch from the edges, stitch the long edges of the strips together, alternating prints and strip widths, using the 4-thread overlock. *Note: Avoid stretching the fleece as you stitch.*

2. Press the seams to one side using a press cloth and low heat. High heat will melt the fleece.

3. Place the throw flat on a large cutting surface. Trim the ends straight and square the corners.

4. Overlock the edges, trimming ¼ inch as you stitch.

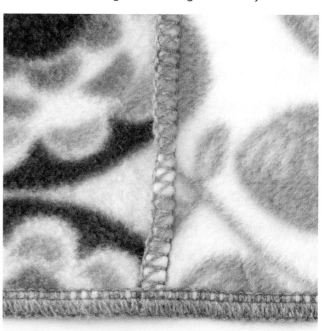

5. Press the edges flat using a press cloth and low temperature. ❖

Credits: *Ty Pennington Impressions fleece fabrics from Westminster Fabrics; YLI Corp. serger yarn; Elite serger threads.*

Wave Valance

Designer's Notes

The wavy, shaped bottom of this easy-to-make valance will give new life to your window treatment. Using a serger not only makes this a fast project, it dresses up the valance with a decorative finish at the edges.

Serger Skill Level
Beginning

Finished Size
Custom

Serger Skills
4-thread overcast seams and edge finishes, serging curves

Materials
- Fabric of choice for valance and borders *(See instructions for determining valance size and yardages.)*
- Drapery lining fabric *(See instructions for determining valance yardage and use the same for the lining.)*
- 3-inch-wide drapery header tape in length to match finished valance width
- Tassel trim equal to valance width
- 2½-inch-diameter curtain grommets
- Wavy ruler (optional)
- Self-adhesive, double-sided basting tape
- Disappearing or water-soluble marker
- Basic sewing supplies and equipment

Threads
- 2 spools serger thread
- 2 spools coordinating rayon thread

Serger Stitches & Settings
Note: *These are suggested serger settings. Be sure to test your stitch on a scrap of project or similar fabric to ensure stitch perfection before beginning your project.*

4-thread overlock for seams and edges
Stitch Length: 2.5
Left Needle Tension: 6
Right Needle Tension: 4
Upper Looper Tension: 4
Lower Looper Tension: 4

Machine Threading
Serger thread in both needles

Rayon thread in both loopers

Determining Valance Size & Yardages
1. Measure the window width from the inside or outside edges of your window frame.

2. The finished width of the valance is 1½ times the measurement from step 1. To allow for seam allowances, cut your fabric 1 inch wider than the finished width. To add a border as shown, or to piece a valance that is wider than the fabric width, add ½-inch seam allowances when figuring yardage and cutting. The borders shown are 5 inches wide.

3. The finished length of the valance is 13 inches as shown; adjust to make it shorter or longer as desired. To determine the cut length, add ½ inch for the bottom seam and 3 inches for a header to the finished length.

4. Use the cut width and length to determine the yardage needed for the valance, border and lining fabrics, and trim. You will need enough grommets to space every 4 to 6 inches across the width.

Cutting & Assembly

1. Using the measurements calculated for your valance, cut a rectangle the determined measurements from the valance, border and lining fabric.

2. With right sides together, use a ½-inch seam allowance and serge the border strips to the ends of the valance panel. Press the seam allowances toward the borders.

3. On the right side of the valance, position the wavy ruler along the lower edge and use a disappearing marker to mark the outline across the valance. If you do not have a wavy ruler, use the marker to draw a wavy line across the bottom edge of the valance tracing the edge of a plate. Cut along the marked line.

4. Align the sides and top edges of the lining and valance fabric, right sides together. Trim the lining to match the wavy edge of the valance fabric.

5. Cut the length of decorative trim ½ inch longer than the valance bottom. If the trim has tassels or brush fringe that are basted together, be careful not to let the basting thread unravel after you cut your trim.

6. To attach the trim, place the valance fabric right side up. Apply basting tape along the bottom edge.

7. Starting in the center, place the trim right sides together along the valance bottom with the edge even with the fabric edge and the trim facing away from you. Leave the extra ½ inch of trim on each side—it will be cut and finished when you serge the ends (Figure 1).

Figure 1

8. With right sides together and edges even, serge the valance to the lining along the bottom edge, trimming ¼ inch as you stitch and keeping the trim away from the seam. ***Note:*** *As you stitch the curves, pay careful attention to keep the stitch width consistent.* Press the edge and turn right side out.

9. With wrong sides together, overlock the sides and top edges of the valance and lining, trimming ¼ inch as you serge. ***Note:*** *Serging the sides will cut the trim at the sides and fasten it securely in the serged seam.*

Making the Header

1. On the lining side of the valance, serge one edge of the drapery header tape to the top edge of the valance.

2. Using the bottom edge of the header tape as a guide, fold the header down and press.

3. Topstitch the header in place, ½ inch from the bottom edge using sewing machine.

4. On the right side of the valance, begin 2 inches from each end and mark evenly spaced grommet placements centered on the header. Follow the manufacturer's instructions to apply the grommets. ❖

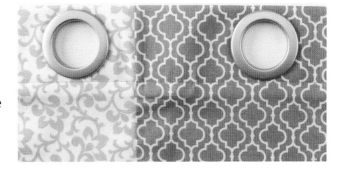

Credits: *Robert Kaufman Metro Living Collection fabrics; June Tailor wave ruler; Expo International #IR6610CCC Cross Ball Trim; Dritz Home curtain grommets.*

Springtime Table Set

Flat Lock Fringe Place Mats

Designer's Notes
Add a designer touch to pieced place mats when you add rayon flat locking to provide a border for the fringe.

Serger Skill Level
Beginner

Finished Size
14 x 19 inches

Serger Skills
3-thread wide overlock, decorative flat locking

Materials for One Place Mat
- ½ yard linen solid
- ⅛ yard each 3 coordinating 100-percent cotton prints
- Permanent fabric adhesive
- Chalk pencil or water-soluble marker
- Basic sewing supplies and equipment

Threads
- 3 spools rayon thread to match linen fabric

Serger Stitches & Settings
Note: These are suggested serger settings. Be sure to test your stitch on a scrap of project or similar fabric to ensure stitch perfection before beginning your project.

3-thread wide overlock for seams
Stitch Length: 2.5
Left Needle Tension: 3
Right Needle: Removed
Upper Looper Tension: 3
Lower Looper Tension: 4

3-thread flat lock for decorative stitching
Stitch Length: 3
Left Needle Tension: 0–1
Right Needle: Removed
Upper Looper Tension: 3
Lower Looper Tension: 6

Optional for flat locking on fold: Foot to protect fabric from cutting blade or disengage cutting blade

Machine Threading
Rayon thread in needle and both loopers

Cutting
From the linen solid:
Cut two 1 x 13½-inch strips for the top and bottom borders.

Cut two 3¼ x 14½-inch strips for the side borders.

Cut one 14½ x 19-inch rectangle for the back.

Tip for Success

When cutting linen for fringing, be sure to cut on the straight grain to ensure even fringing.

From two of the cotton prints:
Cut one 3¾ x 13½-inch strip from each print.

From the remaining cotton print:
Cut two 3¾ x 13½-inch strips.

Assembly
Sew seams right sides together using ¼-inch seam allowance.

1. Using a 3-thread wide overlock, serge the long edges of the 3¾ x 13½-inch cotton print strips together, beginning and ending with the same print to make the pieced center. Press the seams in one direction.

2. Serge the 1 x 13½-inch borders to the top and bottom edges of the pieced center (Figure 1).

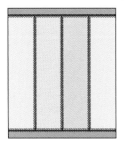

Figure 1

3. Serge the 3¼ x 14½-inch side borders to each side of the pieced center (Figure 2), completing the place mat top. Press the seams toward the center.

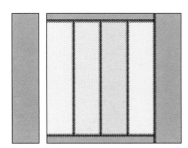

Figure 2

4. With right sides together, serge the pieced front to the back along the top and bottom edges, leaving the side edges open (Figure 3). Turn right side out and press.

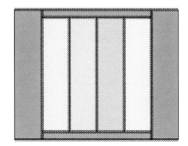

Figure 3

Flat Lock Fringe

1. Using a chalk pencil or water-soluble marker, mark a line on each side border, 1½ inches from the pieced center (Figure 4).

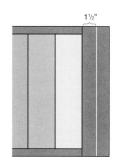

Figure 4

2. Press the border strips under along the marked line.

3. Set the serger for flat locking. Flat lock along each fold, making sure half of the stitch width extends beyond the fold (Figure 5).

Figure 5

4. Pull the stitches flat and press.

5. On the back of the place mat, pull 1 inch of the thread ends under the ladder stitches on each end and secure with a very thin layer of fabric adhesive. Trim excess thread tails.

Tip for Success

Leave long thread tails at the beginning and end of the flat-lock seams to prevent the needle thread from pulling out when securing ends in ladder stitches on reverse.

5. Open the border side seams up to within ¼ inch of the flat locking along border width (Figure 6). Secure seam with fabric adhesive.

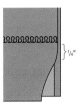

Figure 6

6. To create the fringe, remove the vertical threads to within ¼ inch of the flat locking.

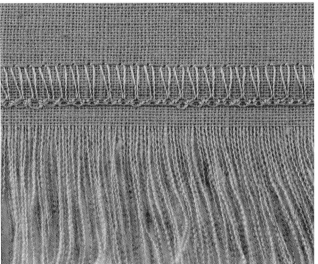

Credits: *Robert Kaufman Essex Linen and Double Happiness Collection cotton print fabrics; Sulky rayon threads; Beacon Adhesives™ Fabri-Tac® permanent fabric adhesive.*

Rolled Edge Napkins

Finished Size
20 x 20 inches

Designer's Notes
Why buy fabric napkins when it's so easy to make your own? Whether you piece them as shown or cut a simple square of fabric, a rolled hem adds a quick, professional-looking finish.

Serger Skills
3-thread wide overcast stitching, rolled edge hem, outside square corners

Materials for One Napkin
- 44/45-inch-wide 100-percent cotton fabrics to match three place mat fabrics:
    - ½ yard of one print
    - ⅛ yard each of remaining two prints
- Seam sealant
- Basic sewing supplies and equipment

Threads
- 2 cones serger thread
- 1 spool coordinating rayon thread

Serger Stitches & Settings
Note: These are suggested serger settings. Be sure to test your stitch on a scrap of project or similar fabric to ensure stitch perfection before beginning your project.

3-thread wide overlock for seams
Stitch Length: 2.5
Left Needle Tension: 3
Right Needle: Removed
Upper Looper Tension: 3
Lower Looper Tension: 4

3-thread rolled edge
Stitch Length: 1.0–2.0
Left Needle: Removed
Right Needle Tension: 3
Upper Looper Tension: 3
Lower Looper Tension: 6
Adjustments for rolled edge: Use rolled-edge stitch finger

Machine Threading
Overlock: serger thread in needle and both loopers

Rolled edge: serger thread in needle and lower looper, and rayon thread in upper looper

Cutting
From the ½ yard print:
Cut one 16¼ x 20¼-inch rectangle.

From each ⅛ yard print:
Cut one 2½ x 20¼-inch strip.

Assembly
Serge seams with right sides together using a ¼-inch seam allowance.

1. Use a 3-thread wide overlock to serge the long edges of the 2½ x 20¼-inch fabric strips together. Press seam allowances to one side.

2. Serge the pieced strips to one long edge of the rectangle. Press the seam allowance in the same direction as the pieced strips.

Rolled-Edge Hem
1. Beginning at one corner, serge across one edge of the fabric, slightly trimming the edge. Stop several stitches from the next corner.

2. Turn the hand wheel until you have made one stitch past the corner. Raise the presser foot and needle, and pull a small amount of slack in the needle thread. Carefully slip the fabric off the stitch finger and turn it so the next edge is ready to stitch. Make sure there isn't too much fabric slack or you will have a loop at the corner.

3. Place the needle down in the fabric at the edge of the stitching and serge the next edge.

Tips for Success

Practice stitching the rolled edge on scraps of the project fabric to determine the best settings.

If the top thread doesn't meet the needle thread on the underside, slightly tighten the lower looper tension.

If there are loops on the top or edge of your fabric, slightly tighten the upper looper tension.

You may need to tighten the upper looper tension when using rayon thread or woolly nylon thread.

4. Repeat steps 1 to 3 until all four edges are hemmed.

5. Gently pull the thread chain to straighten the threads and trim to 2 inches long.

6. Thread the chain through the eye of a tapestry needle and slide the thread chain ½ inch under the stitches on the underside of the napkin.

7. Apply a dab of seam sealant to secure. Trim the thread chain when the seam sealant is dry. ❖

Credits: *Robert Kaufman Double Happiness cotton print fabrics; Sulky rayon and 30 wt. cotton threads.*

Cute Kitty Baby Mat

Designer's Notes
Mom and baby alike will love this warm and fuzzy floor mat. Shaped like a kitty, it is made of cuddle fabric, and the edges are serged with woolly nylon thread for a soft finish.

Serger Skill Level
Beginning

Finished Size
25 x 36 inches

Serger Skills
Finishing edges, serging curves and corners, working with deep-pile fabric

Materials
- ¾ yard pink cuddle fabric
- ½ yard white cuddle fabric
- ¾ yard coordinating cotton polka-dot fabric
- 8½ x 11-inch sheet double-stick fusible web
- Scrap black flannel
- Pattern-tracing paper or fabric
- Lightweight water-soluble stabilizer
- Permanent fabric adhesive
- Fabric basting spray
- Press cloth
- Basic sewing equipment and supplies

Threads
- 3 spools serger thread
- 1 spool woolly nylon thread
- Coordinating all-purpose sewing thread

Serger Stitches & Settings
Note: These are suggested serger settings. Be sure to test your stitch on a scrap of project or similar fabric to ensure stitch perfection before beginning your project.

3-thread wide overlock for edges
Stitch Length: 3.0
Left Needle Tension: 4
Right Needle: Removed
Upper Looper Tension: 1
Lower Looper Tension: 4
Adjustments for deep-pile fabric:
Increase cutting/stitch width to 6.

Machine Threading
Serger thread in both needles and lower looper

Woolly nylon thread in upper looper (tension reduced)

Cutting
Enlarge and trace the head and arm/leg patterns provided on page 55 onto pattern-tracing paper or fabric to make templates, following instructions on patterns.

From the pink cuddle fabric:
Cut one 26-inch-diameter circle.

Using templates, cut one head and four arm/leg pieces.

From the white cuddle fabric:
Cut one 18-inch-diameter circle.

From the polka-dot fabric:
Cut one 26-inch-diameter circle.

Using templates, cut one head and four arm/leg pieces.

Face Appliqué
1. Using the facial features on the head pattern, trace two each cheeks, eyes and inner ears, and one nose onto the fusible web paper backing, leaving at least ½ inch between each.

2. Cut out fusible web appliqué pieces leaving a ¼-inch margin around each.

3. Following manufacturer's instructions, fuse the cheeks, nose and inner ears fusible web appliqué pieces to the wrong side of the polka-dot fabric.

4. Fuse the eyes to the wrong side of the black flannel.

5. Cut out the facial-feature appliqués along the drawn lines.

6. Referring to the pattern for placement, remove the backing from the appliqué shapes and position them on the cuddle-fabric head piece. Use a press cloth and fuse the appliqués in place. *Note: Do not apply the iron directly to the cuddle fleece fabric as it will melt. Use a press cloth and a medium heat setting to press.*

Bb

for bear

Cc

for cat

7. Cover the appliqué shapes with lightweight water-soluble stabilizer and use sewing machine to zigzag-stitch over the edges of each shape with matching thread.

Tips for Success

Use lightweight water-soluble stabilizer on top of deep-pile fabrics to prevent the stitches from sinking into the pile and disappearing when stitching highlights or embroidery.

If you are having trouble with a lofty fabric, trim more to get a clean cut. Add another ¼-inch seam allowance to do this. If you are still having problems getting through a high loft, use your sewing machine to sew a straight stitch ¼ inch from the edge. Guide the fabric so your knife cuts along the stitched line. This will clear the way for the looper threads to meet the needle and create a nice stitch.

8. Gently tear the stabilizer away from the stitches. Use tweezers to remove from under the stitches, if needed.

9. Trace the mouth and whiskers onto water-soluble stabilizer and position on the face. Stitch over the lines using a zigzag stitch. Carefully remove the stabilizer.

Body Assembly

1. Apply basting spray to wrong side of white cuddle circle following manufacturer's instructions.

2. Center the white cuddle circle on the right side of the pink cuddle circle.

3. Use sewing machine and a wide, open zigzag stitch to stitch the edges of the white circle in place.

4. Align each pink cuddle piece with its corresponding polka-dot piece, wrong sides together. Pin the pieces together at least 1 inch from the edge.

5. Serge the edges of each pair of pieces together. Pull the thread tails under the stitches on the polka-dot side and secure with a dab of fabric adhesive; trim. Press each piece on the polka-dot side.

Completing Mat

1. Place the pink cuddle side of circle right side up on a flat surface. Position the head at the top of the circle, overlapping the circle edge by 2 to 3 inches (Figure 1). Pin and sew in place using sewing machine.

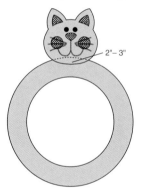

2"– 3"

Figure 1

2. To add an arm, position an arm/leg piece 4½ inches from one side of the head with the circle overlapping the arm/leg piece by 1 inch (Figure 2). Pin in place to hold.

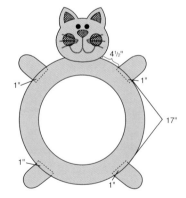

4½" 1" 1" 17" 1" 1"

Figure 2

3. Repeat step 2 to add another arm to the opposite side of the head.

4. To add legs, position and pin a remaining arm/leg piece 17 inches from an arm with the circle overlapping the arm/leg piece by 1 inch, again referring to Figure 2. Repeat on opposite side.

5. Use sewing machine to stitch all overlapping edges in place as shown in Figure 3a and Figure 3b. ❖

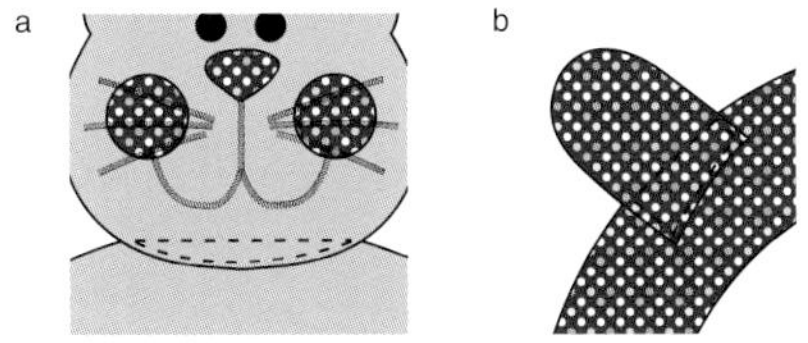

Figure 3

Credits: *Shannon Fabrics Cuddle Fabric; Robert Kaufman cotton print fabric; YLI woolly nylon and Elite serger threads; Warm Company Steam-a-Seam 2® Fusible Web; Sulky® Solvy™ stabilizer; Beacon Adhesives™ Fabri-Tac® permanent fabric adhesive.*

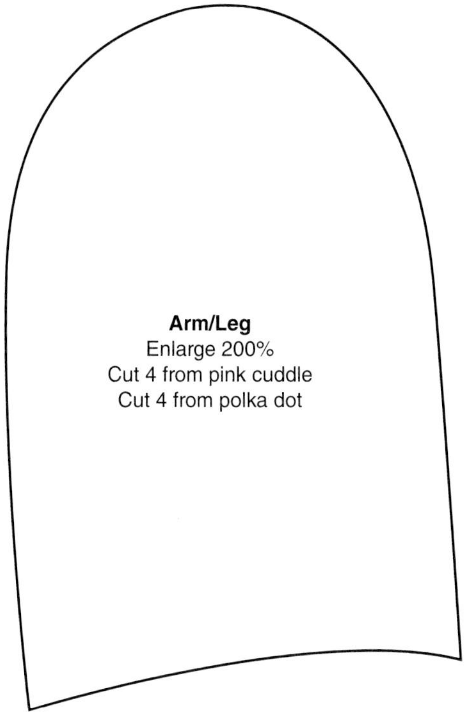

Arm/Leg
Enlarge 200%
Cut 4 from pink cuddle
Cut 4 from polka dot

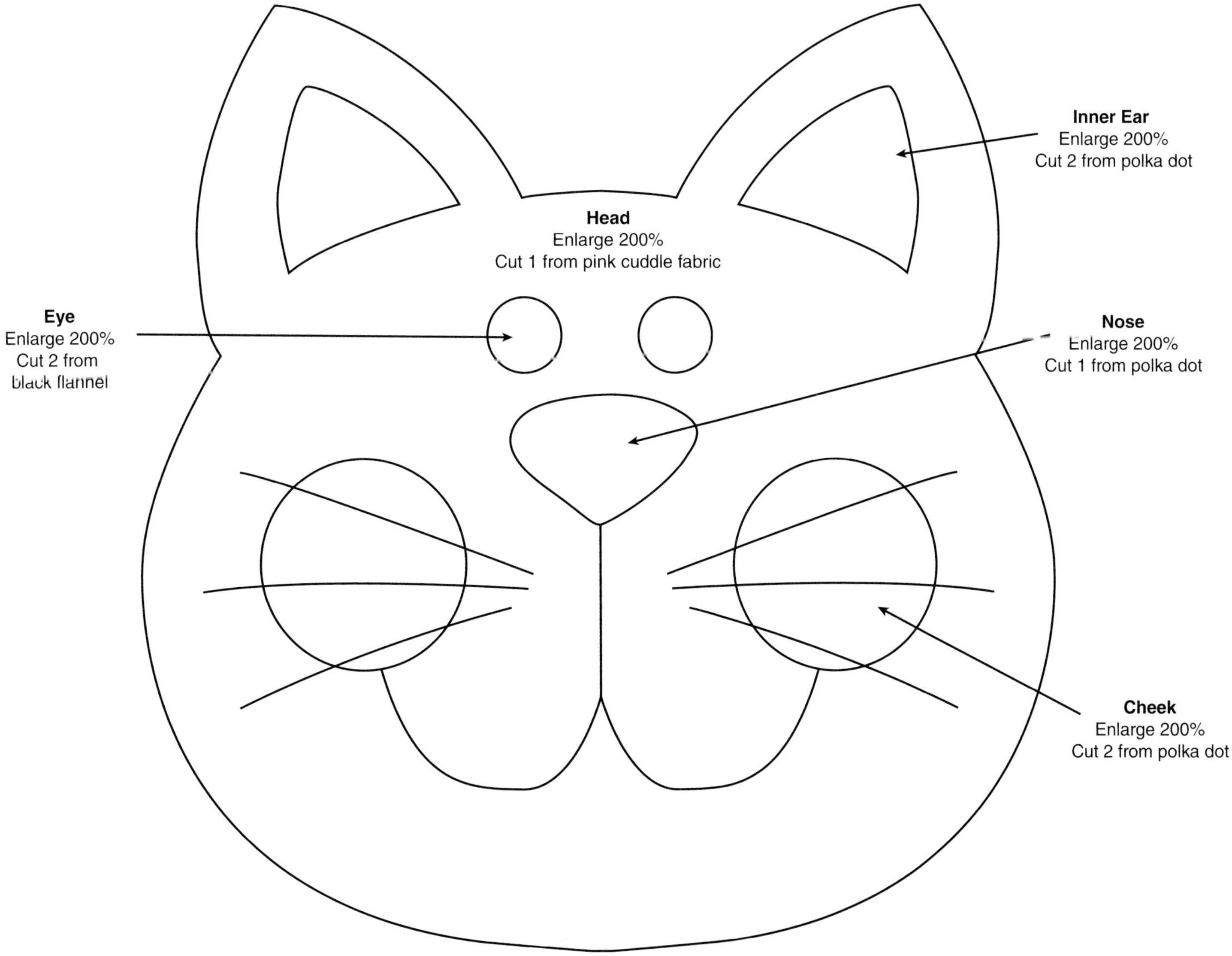

Inner Ear
Enlarge 200%
Cut 2 from polka dot

Head
Enlarge 200%
Cut 1 from pink cuddle fabric

Eye
Enlarge 200%
Cut 2 from
black flannel

Nose
Enlarge 200%
Cut 1 from polka dot

Cheek
Enlarge 200%
Cut 2 from polka dot

Rose Garden Kitchen Set

Casserole Carrier

Designer's Notes
Tote a casserole or pan of brownies to the next potluck in style with this quilted carrier. Using reversible quilted fabric and your serger make it a super-fast project that will impress friends and family. The optional top attaches with hook-and-loop tape, and the sturdy handles let you carry even the heaviest casseroles worry-free. The featured size will hold a dish up to 9 x 13 inches. Simply adjust the cutting dimensions to make a different size.

Serger Skill Level
Intermediate

Finished Size
10 x 14 x 3 inches

Serger Skills
4-thread wide overlock seams, edge finish, attaching binding, serging curves

Materials
- 44/45-inch-wide 100-percent cotton fabric:
  1 yard reversible quilted fabric
  ½ yard coordinating print fabric for binding
- 1⅛ yards ⅜-inch-wide elastic
- Hook-and-loop tape (optional)
- Basic sewing tools and equipment

Threads
- 2 cones 30 wt. solid-color cotton serger thread
- 1 cone 30 wt. variegated cotton serger thread
- All-purpose coordinating sewing thread

Tip for Success

One of the advantages of using reversible fabric, in addition to eliminating the need for lining, is that you can use either side as the outside of your project. For the carrier, you can mix it up, using one side out for the sides and base, and the other side out for the handles.

Serger Stitches & Settings
***Note:** These are suggested serger settings. Be sure to test your stitch on a scrap of project or similar fabric to ensure stitch perfection before beginning your project.*

4-thread wide overlock for seams & edges
Stitch Length: 2.5
Left Needle Tension: 3
Right Needle Tension: 3
Upper Looper Tension: 3
Lower Looper Tension: 4

Machine Threading
Solid-color thread in needle and loopers

Variegated thread in upper looper (optional for decorative edge on handles and cover)

Cutting
From the quilted fabric:
Cut one 11 x 15-inch rectangle for bottom A.

Cut one 13 x 17-inch rectangle for top B.

Cut two 4 x 11-inch strips for short sides C.

Cut two 4 x 15-inch strips for long sides D.

Cut two 5 x 36-inch strips for handles E.

From the coordinating print:
Cut one 14-inch square. Cut square into 2½-inch bias strips.

Assembly

Carrier body
Assemble with right sides together using a ½-inch seam allowance unless otherwise indicated. As you are serging, cut ¼-inch from the seam. Because the fabric is bulky, you will need that much fabric to the right of your blade to get a nice, clean cut.

1. Using a wide 4-thread overlock stitch, serge a C and D rectangle right sides together along one short edge, stopping ½ inch from the end. Trim ¼-inch from the edge of the fabric where you

haven't serged it so the unserged seam allowance is even with the serged seam allowance.

Figure 1

2. Repeat step 1, serging the remaining C and D strips together alternately to make the casserole carrier sides, referring to Figure 2.

Figure 2

3. Align the bottom rectangle A with the side seams and serge the carrier sides to carrier bottom A, matching side seams to A corners as shown in Figure 3. You will need to again trim ¼-inch as you serge to get a clean cut. Begin serging at one long end, making sure you are serging close to the base of the side at the corner. Serge off at the next corner. Turn the fabric and begin serging the shorter edge until you reach the next corner and then serge off. Do the same for the remaining sides. Set aside.

Figure 3

Binding

1. Overlock bias strips together on short ends. Press seams in one direction.

2. Press one short end to wrong side ½ inch. Then press both long sides ⅝ inch to center. Press bias strip in half lengthwise to make a double-folded bias tape (Figure 4).

Figure 4

3. Open the binding. Beginning with the folded short end positioned at the center of one side, overlock one raw binding edge to the outside of the carrier side, keeping edges even and overlapping ends. Refold the binding to the inside of the carrier.

4. Using the sewing machine, edgestitch the binding in place, leaving an opening to insert elastic (Figure 5).

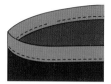

Figure 5

5. Using a loop turner, insert the ⅜-inch-wide elastic into the opening and pull evenly through the binding.

6. Overlap the elastic ends and sew together. Push back into the binding opening and edgestitch the opening closed.

Handles

1. Serge the handles, trimming close to the edges so you have just the ¼-inch of the serged stitches along each long side of the two handle pieces E. (Put variegated thread in the upper looper if you want these edges finished with a decorative touch.)

2. Mark handle placement lines at the center of the carrier bottom A width and 3 inches in from both short ends (Figure 6).

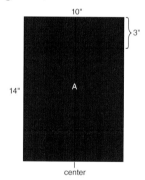

Figure 6

3. Overlap handle ends ½ inch and stitch together with the sewing machine with one line of stitching at each fabric end as shown in Figure 7a and 7b.

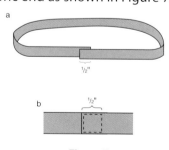

Figure 7

4. Position and pin handles E at the placement lines with overlapping ends at the centerline (Figure 8).

Figure 8

5. Using sewing machine, edgestitch handles to carrier bottom and sides, referring again to Figure 8.

Optional Cover

1. To make a cover, trace around a small lid or cup positioned in the corners of the B rectangle to round the corners.

2. Overlock all the edges, trimming off the corners along the drawn line. Put variegated thread in the upper looper for a decorative touch.

3. If desired, position and sew squares or circles of hook-and-loop tape at the centers of all four sides of both the cover and carrier sides to secure the cover when in use.

Credits: Fabri-Quilt Sweet Garden collection fabrics; Sulky variegated and solid-color cotton serger threads.

Yo-Yo Flowers Hand Towel

Designer's Notes
Making yo-yos is a snap when you use a serger. Finish the edge of a fabric circle with overcast stitches positioned over pearl cotton thread; then just draw up the pearl cotton thread and you have easy gathering. Make one or a dozen to embellish towels, pillows and more. This whimsical hand towel is finished with a ruffle that was gathered using the same technique and hemmed with a rolled edge.

Finished Size
16 x 24 inches

Serger Skills
3-thread wide overlock edge finish, rolled edge hem on ruffle, overlock gathering, turning corners

Materials
- 44/45-inch-wide 100-percent cotton fabric:
    ½ yard waffle cloth
    ⅛ yard coordinating print
- 2 (7-inch square) scraps cotton prints
- ½ yard ½-inch-wide grosgrain ribbon
- 1 yard ¼-inch-wide fusible decorative bias tape
- 2 (¾-inch-diameter) buttons
- Water-soluble basting tape
- Permanent fabric adhesive
- Basic sewing supplies and equipment

Threads
- 2 cones 30 wt. solid-color cotton serger thread
- 1 cone 30 wt. variegated cotton serger thread
- 1 spool pearl cotton
- All-purpose sewing thread to match ribbon

Serger Stitches & Settings

Note: These are suggested serger settings. Be sure to test your stitch on a scrap of project or similar fabric to ensure stitch perfection before beginning your project.

3-thread wide overlock for seams & edges
Stitch Length: 2.5
Left Needle Tension: 3
Right Needle: Removed
Upper Looper Tension: 3
Lower Looper Tension: 4

3-thread rolled edge
Stitch Length: 1.0
Left Needle: Removed
Right Needle Tension: 3
Upper Looper Tension: 3
Lower Looper Tension: 6

Adjustments for rolled edge: Use rolled-edge stitch finger or drop stitch finger. (Check owner's manual.)

Machine Threading
Solid-color thread in needle and lower looper

Variegated thread in upper looper

Cutting
From waffle cloth:
Cut one 16 x 20-inch rectangle for towel body.

From coordinating print:
Cut one 4-inch-wide strip across the width of the fabric for the ruffle.

From print scraps:
Cut one 6-inch-diameter circle and one 7-inch-diameter circle for the yo-yo flowers.

Towel Assembly
Use ¼-inch seam allowances unless otherwise indicated.

1. With a 3-thread wide overlock, finish the side and top edges of the waffle cloth rectangle. This is a perfect opportunity to practice your serger technique for turning corners. Also serge the short edges of the ruffle strip and the ribbon ends.

2. Being careful not to catch the thread in the stitching, overlock over the pearl cotton thread along one long edge of the ruffle (Figure 1).

Figure 1

3. Finish one long edge of the ruffle with a rolled edge hem, slightly trimming the edge as you serge.

4. Hand-stitch one end of the pearl cotton through the fabric at the end of the stitching and knot securely. Pull the pearl cotton ends to gather the ruffle edge to 16 inches. Stitch the end through the fabric and knot securely.

5. Position the ruffle-gathered edge right sides together and even with the bottom edge of the waffle cloth. Evenly arrange the gathers and serge the edges together with a 3-thread wide overlock.

6. Press the seam allowance toward towel and baste in place.

Making the Yo-Yos

1. Finish the edge of each fabric circle with a 3-thread wide overlock, stitching over a pearl cotton thread. Follow the instructions on previous page for gathering ruffle to gather edges of circles. Be sure to leave long tails of pearl cotton thread at both ends.

2. Pull the pearl cotton thread ends to tightly gather the edge. Knot the thread ends together securely.

3. Flatten gathered circle with gathered edge at the center.

4. Position and pin the yo-yos in the center third of the towel front, 6 inches and 4 inches from the top of the ruffle and 4½ inches from each side (Figure 2).

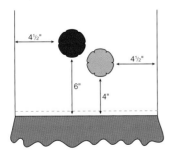

Figure 2

Making Stems & Leaves

1. Cut 6½-inch and 4½-inch lengths of fusible bias tape for stems and three 6-inch lengths for leaves.

2. Position and pin stem pieces ½ inch under yo-yos and touching top of ruffle. Don't fuse in place until leaves are in place.

3. Refer to the project photo and Figure 3 to shape the 6-inch bias pieces into leaves. Position and pin under flower stems, again referring to Figure 3. Fuse leaves and stems in place following manufacturer's instructions.

Figure 3

Tip for Success

Use water-soluble basting tape instead of pins to secure project pieces together for serging. Pieces will be held firmly in place, and your hands are free for guiding your project through the serger.

Finishing the Towel

1. Center and pin the ribbon length over ruffle seam. Fold ends to wrong side and pin.

2. Using a sewing machine, topstitch the ribbon edge to towel with coordinating thread.

3. Hand-stitch ¾-inch buttons to yo-yo centers to complete. Sewing the buttons will permanently attach the yo-yos to the towel.

Credits: *Fabri-Quilt Sweet Garden collection fabrics; James Thompson waffle cloth; Sulky variegated and solid-color cotton serger thread; Clover Quick Bias fusible bias tape; Blumenthal Lansing buttons.*

Oven Mitt

Designer's Note
This oven mitt is practical as well as pretty.

Finished Size
7½ x 12½ inches

Serger Skills
3-thread wide overlock seams, rolled-edge hem on ruffle, overlock for gathering

Materials
- 44/45-inch wide 100-percent cotton fabric
  - ⅓ yard reversible quilted fabric
  - ⅜ yard coordinating print fabric for lining and ruffle
- ¼ yard Insul-Bright or other insulating heat-resistant material
- ⅓ yard ½-inch-wide grosgrain ribbon
- Flower buttons: 2 (½-inch), 1 (¾-inch)
- Tracing paper
- Seam sealant
- Basic sewing supplies and equipment

Threads
- 2 cones 30 wt. solid-color cotton serger thread
- 1 cone 30 wt. variegated cotton serger thread
- 1 spool pearl cotton
- All-purpose coordinating sewing thread

Serger Stitches & Settings
3-thread wide overlock for seams & edges
Stitch Length: 2.5
Left Needle Tension: 3
Right Needle: Removed
Upper Looper Tension: 3
Lower Looper Tension: 4

3-thread rolled edge
Stitch Length: 1.0
Left Needle: Removed
Right Needle Tension: 3
Upper Looper Tension: 3
Lower Looper Tension: 6

Adjustments for rolled edge: Use rolled-edge stitch finger or lower your stitch finger.
(Check your owner's manual.)

Machine Threading
Solid-color thread in needle and lower looper

Variegated thread in upper looper

Cutting
Trace the mitt pattern (page 64) onto tracing paper to make a template. Use template to cut mitts as follows:

From the quilted fabric
Using the pattern, cut out two mitts, reversing one.

From the coordinating print
Cut two mitts for linings, reversing one.

Cut one 2½ x 38-inch strip for the ruffle.

From the Insul-Bright
Cut two mitts, reversing one.

Assembly
Use a ¼-inch seam allowance unless otherwise indicated.

Ruffle
1. Finish one long edge of the 2½ x 38-inch ruffle strip with a 3-thread rolled edge, slightly trimming the fabric.

2. On the opposite raw edge, use a wide 3-thread overlock and stitch over a pearl cotton thread being careful not to catch the pearl cotton in the stitching and leaving long ends at both the beginning and end of the seam (Figure 1).

Figure 1

3. Lay out oven mitt pieces, right side down and thumbs to the outside, similar to Figure 4.

4. Place Insul-Bright, shiny side down, on top of each mitt piece.

5. Place lining pieces, right side up, on top of Insul-Bright.

6. Hand or machine baste close to the edges through all layers of the front and back oven mitt pieces to prepare for serging.

7. Place front and back pieces together with quilted fabric sides facing. Overlock oven mitt front and back pieces approximately 4 inches up the side seam from the lower edge (Figure 2).

4"

Figure 2

8. Open oven mitt flat. Apply basting tape to bottom edge of quilted side of mitt. Remove basting-tape paper. Position grosgrain ribbon over basting tape, matching edge to mitt bottom edge (Figure 3).

Figure 3

9. With right side of ruffle facing quilted side of mitt, pin center of ruffle to mitt seam and ruffle ends to mitt ends over ribbon. Pull pearl cotton at ruffle edges to gather evenly along oven mitt edge. Pin to secure (Figure 4). Trim pearl cotton ends to 3 inches long.

Figure 4

10. Overlock mitt bottom edge through all layers. Trim ribbon and pearl cotton short ends even with mitt sides.

11. Press seam toward mitt. Using thread to match quilting of mitt fabric, topstitch seam with sewing machine (Figure 5).

Figure 5

64

12. Complete overlocking oven mitt side seams, matching edges and bottom seam (Figure 6). Clip thumb curve if necessary for easy turning. Turn right side out.

Figure 6

13. Sew ½-inch buttons on ribbon at side seams (Figure 7).

Figure 7

14. Sew ¾-inch button on ribbon at center of front of oven mitt, again referring to Figure 7, to complete the oven mitt. ❖

Credits: Fabri-Quilt Sweet Garden collection fabrics; Sulky variegated and solid-color cotton serger thread; Blumenthal Lansing flower buttons.

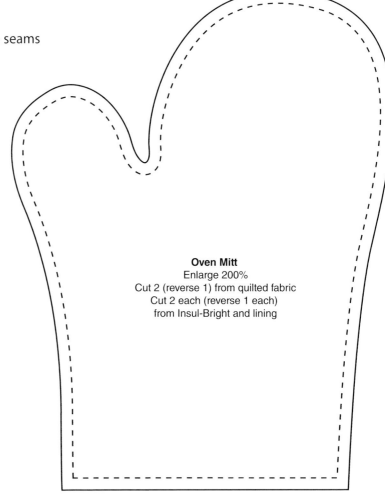

Oven Mitt
Enlarge 200%
Cut 2 (reverse 1) from quilted fabric
Cut 2 each (reverse 1 each)
from Insul-Bright and lining

Heirloom Lace Pillowcase

Designer's Notes

I love antique linens and am the third generation to inherit a bag of my great-grandmother's laces and fine embroidered fabrics. Instead of continuing to pass on the bag, I decided to piece together some of my favorites for a pillow cover using fine heirloom serging. You can use any combination of laces, entredeux (pieces of light-weight embroidered fabric or ribbon joined together with lace), ribbons and lightweight embroidered fabric like silk batiste or organza—antique or new—to create a similar look. If you choose a plain fabric, consider adding serger pintucks to complement the look.

Thanks to the adjustments you can make in serger settings, a delicate look is easy to create by using very narrow seams and two threads. For the featured pillow cover, I used a flat lock and changed the needle position to adjust the width.

Serger Skill Level
Intermediate

Finished Size
15 x 27 inches

Serger Skills
2-thread flat lock for piecing, 3-thread narrow over-lock for pillow top construction and back edge finish

Materials
- 1 yard 44/45-inch-wide silk or cotton batiste fabric
- Insertions: 18-inch lengths of assorted laces or fabrics to total 27 inches wide: ⅛-inch-wide ribbons, entredeux trim, embroidered trim or lightweight fabrics
- 14 x 18-inch pillow form
- Basic sewing supplies and equipment

Threads
- 3 spools coordinating rayon thread
- 3 spools coordinating serger thread

Serger Stitches & Settings
Note: These are suggested serger settings. Be sure to test your stitch on a scrap of project or similar fabric to ensure stitch perfection before beginning your project.

2-thread flat lock for heirloom piecing
Stitch Length: 1.5–3, depending on technique
Left Needle (or Right Needle) Tension: 0–3, depending on technique
Upper Looper: Disengaged (Refer to your owner's manual.)
Lower Looper Tension: 5

3-thread narrow overlock for pillowcase & cover seams
Stitch Length: 2
Left Needle: Removed
Right Needle Tension: 3
Upper Looper Tension: 4
Lower Looper Tension: 4

Machine Threading
Rayon thread in needle and lower looper for flat lock

Rayon thread in needle and both loopers for 3-thread narrow overlock

Cutting
From the batiste fabric:
Cut two 15 x 19-inch rectangles for the pillow cover.

Cut one 16 x 27-inch rectangle for the pillowcase back. **Note:** *For a more fitted pillowcase, cut the pillow-case back 15 x 27 inches.*

Pillow Top Heirloom Piecing
1. Arrange assorted 18-inch lengths of insertion materials side by side to at least 27 inches wide.

2. To join fabric to fabric or lace with a tightened flat lock, set up a flat lock with the needle in the right position and a needle tension of 3 instead of 0–1. **Note:** *Because the needle tension is tight, the layers won't pull apart as they usually do for a flat lock. A narrow 2-thread seam similar in appearance to an overlock seam is created.*

3. With right sides of the fabrics together, serge along the edge, trimming slightly to prevent the edges from shifting out of the seam.

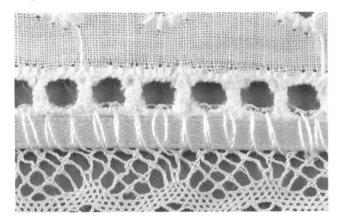

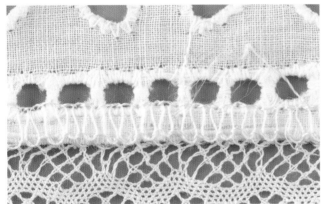

4. To join entredeux trim to lace or fabric, carefully trim the fabric from the embroidery without cutting the embroidered threads.

5. To join to lace, place the entredeux on top of the lace with right sides together and edges even.

6. To join to fabric, place the entredeux on top of the fabric with right sides together and the fabric edge extended slightly for trimming.

7. Set the lower looper tension to 5 and right needle tension to 0–1. Adjust the stitch length so the needle will stitch into the entredeux openings.

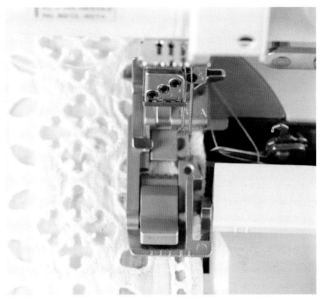

8. To join two pieces of lace with flat locking and ribbon, set up a flat lock with the needle in the left position and needle tension set to 0–1. Set the stitch length at 2.5–3.0.

9. Layer a strip of lace right sides together with a ⅛-inch strip of ribbon and another piece of lace.

10. Stitch along the edges of the lace, encasing the ribbon under the stitches without catching it in the seam.

11. Pull the lace strips flat. The lace edges should overlap, with the ribbon on the top of the overlap. Use a blunt needle to work the ribbon on top of the lace if necessary.

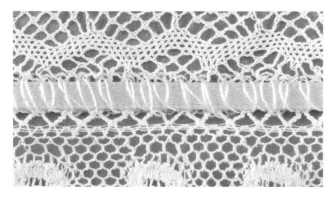

12. To join fabric to lace with ladder side of 2-thread flat lock, set up a regular 2-thread flat lock with a stitch length of 3, left needle tension at 0–1, and lower looper at 5. ***Note:*** *Disengage the blade if possible.*

13. Press the fabric edge to the wrong side ¼ to ½ inch.

14. Layer the fabric and lace with right sides together and flat lock along the edge. ***Note:*** *If your blade does not disengage, stitch along the edge without cutting.*

15. To have the lace overlap the fabric edge under the ladder stitches, stitch with the loops barely off the edge. To create a space between the fabric and lace edges, stitch with the loops farther off the edge.

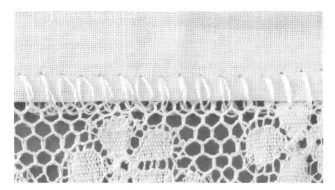

Pillow Construction

1. With right sides together, using a ½-inch seam allowance and 3-thread narrow overlock with regular serger thread, serge the pillow cover panels together. Leave a 10-inch opening in the center of one long edge for turning.

2. Turn the pillow cover right side out and press.

3. Insert the pillow form into the opening and slip-stitch the opening closed.

Pillowcase Assembly

1. The assembled lace panel should be approximately 18 x 27 inches. Trim the top and bottom edges only to make a 16 x 27-inch rectangle.

2. Finish the short edges of the 16 x 27-inch pillowcase back with a 3-thread narrow overlock using regular serger thread.

3. With right sides together, use a 3-thread narrow overlock and ¼-inch seam allowance to serge the top and bottom edges of the lace panel and pillowcase back together. Turn right side out and press.

4. Slide and center the pillowcase onto the pillow. ❖

Credits: *Thai Silks silk batiste fabric; Sulky rayon thread; Fairfield Processing Corp. pillow form.*

T-shirt Quilt

Designer's Notes

Capture school or sports memories when you make a quilt from T-shirts. When my daughter-in-law, Kate, and I were planning this quilt with her college T-shirts, we decided it should have a fun look.

She loves color and so do I, so instead of making a traditional block-and-sashing quilt with the same size blocks and sashing strips, I suggested using unstructured quilt blocks. The blocks are cut in a variety of sizes and the sashing strips are pieced with a cut-as-you-go technique that is especially easy to do with a serger's cutting capabilities.

I used 25 shirt fronts and backs for this full-size quilt, but you can easily make one smaller or larger depending on the number of shirts you'd like to feature.

Serger Skill Level

Intermediate

Finished Size

75 x 85 inches

Serger Skills

3-thread overcast seams, applying and cutting sashing strips, applying binding, turning and mitering corners

Materials

- 44/45-inch-wide 100-percent cotton fabric
    ½ yard each of 6 coordinating prints
    5¼ yards backing fabric
- 25 T-shirt fronts and/or backs
- 6½ yards fusible woven interfacing at least 36 inches wide
- Packaged queen-size quilt batting (84 x 96 inches)
- ¼-inch-wide double-stick fusible web tape
- Square and rectangle clear grid rulers
- Rotary cutter and mat
- Basic sewing supplies and equipment

Threads

- 3 spools coordinating serger thread
- Invisible sewing thread
- All-purpose coordinating sewing thread

Serger Stitches & Settings

Note: These are suggested serger settings. Be sure to test your stitch on a scrap of project or similar fabric to ensure stitch perfection before beginning your project.

3-thread wide overlock

Stitch Length: 2.5
Left Needle Tension: 3
Right Needle: Removed
Upper Looper Tension: 3
Lower Looper Tension: 4

Machine Threading

Serger thread in needle and both loopers

Planning the Quilt

1. Cut the T-shirts in half along the sides and shoulders, cutting around the sleeve and neckline seams.

2. Lay out the T-shirt fronts and/or backs on a large, flat surface and arrange them as desired. Try to alternate colors and logo sizes to achieve a pleasing balance. If you have several small logos, as shown on the center bottom block, these can be pieced together to make a single large block.

3. Draw a plan for your T-shirt placement on graph paper. The quilt shown features five vertical rows of five blocks each. Each block, including sashing strips, is 12–18 inches long and 14–16 inches wide.

4. After you determine the block size, plan the size you want to cut each T-shirt block and the maximum width of your sashing strips, adding ¼-inch seam allowance. *Note: For the unstructured look, vary the widths of the strips and plan to piece some of them at angles as shown in the photo. I mixed these randomly in alternating rows. I also added an extra straight border to the top or bottom edges of some blocks.*

Cutting

1. Cut 25 (16 x 18-inch) rectangles from the fusible interfacing. Fuse a rectangle to the wrong side of each prepared T-shirt front/back.

2. Using your plan as a guide, cut the T-shirt panels to the sizes determined.

3. For the sashing strips, cut 2½-inch by fabric width strips from five of the ½-yard coordinating fabric pieces.

4. Cut the 5¼ yards fabric in half crosswise for backing.

5. Cut 330 inches of 2¼-inch bias strips from the remaining ½ yard of coordinating fabric for binding.

Quilt Block Assembly

1. For each block with straight sashing strips, cut a strip of fabric 1 inch longer than the right edge of the block.

2. With right sides together and using a ¼-inch seam allowance, center and serge the strip to the right edge of the block without trimming the edges with the blade (Figure 1). Press the strip open.

Figure 1

3. Cut a strip 1 inch longer than the bottom edge, including the extra width of the sashing strip. Align this strip with the bottom edge of the block, extending it over the first sashing strip (Figure 2).

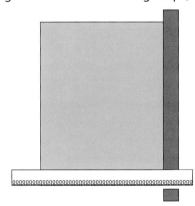

Figure 2

4. Serge along the edge of the strip, cutting off the excess end of the first strip, again referring to Figure 2.

5. Continue adding strips clockwise around the block.

6. Use a clear grid ruler and rotary cutter to trim each block to the determined size including ¼-inch seam allowances.

7. For each block with angle-pieced sashing strips, follow steps 1–6 to add one row of strips around the block.

8. To make angled sashing strips, use a clear ruler and rotary cutter and cut sashing strip as shown in Figure 3.

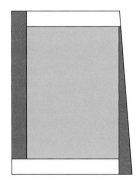

Figure 3

9. Cut a strip that is longer than the strip you just trimmed and serge the long edge to the trimmed strip with the excess length at the widest end of the first strip, referring to Figure 4.

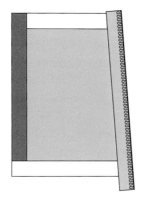

Figure 4

10. Continue to add a second row of strips around the first row, serging them in place and cutting off the excess ends of the underlying strips as in step 4.

11. Use clear grid ruler and align the grid with the straight seams around the T-shirt center. Trim the pieced block to the size determined in step 4 of Planning the Quilt (Figure 5).

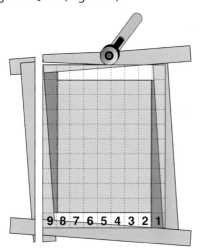

Figure 5

Quilt Top Assembly

1. Referring to your plan, serge the top and bottom edges of the blocks together to assemble each vertical row. Use a ¼-inch seam allowance without trimming the edge.

2. Serge the vertical rows together, without trimming the edges, using a ¼-inch seam allowance.

3. Press all seams. Trim the edges even and square the corners as needed.

Tips for Success

Press seam allowances to the side after stitching.

Make sure crossing seam allowances are flat when you serge over them. Twisted seam allowances will appear as a lump in the seam. If this accidentally happens, clip the seam allowance to lie flat and apply seam sealant to the cut edges.

Completing the Quilt

1. Serge the long edges of the two backing panels together. Press the seam to one side.

2. Cut the batting to the same size as the backing fabric.

3. Lay the backing, wrong side up, on a large flat surface and place the batting on top with the edges even.

4. Center the pieced quilt top on the batting. Beginning in the center, pin the layers together across all pieced block seams and along the edges. *Note: You can also use fabric basting spray to hold the quilt layers together for quilting. Follow manufacturer's instructions and spray-baste the batting to the backing and then the top to the batting.*

5. Using a sewing machine with invisible thread in the needle and thread to match the backing in the bobbin, stitch the layers together in the pieced block seamlines.

6. Baste the edges together and remove all pins. Trim the batting and backing to ¼ inch from the edge of the quilt top.

Binding

1. Serge the short ends of the bias strips together. Press the strip in half lengthwise with wrong sides together.

2. Trim the batting and backing even with the quilt top 1 inch from each corner on each side. Begin in the center of one edge and align the raw edges of the binding strip with the edge of the quilt top. Starting 1 inch from the end of the binding, serge it in place along the edge of the binding and quilt top, trimming off the excess batting and backing (Figure 6)

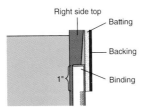

Figure 6

3. To miter each corner, serge to within one stitch of the end of the first edge. Lift the presser foot and needle and gently remove the fabric from the stitch finger. Fold the binding at a 45-degree angle and put the needle back down in the edge one stitch from the corner. Continue serging the binding in place.

4. To join the binding ends, stop stitching several inches from the beginning end, leaving the needle down in the fabric and the presser foot down. Trim the end of the strip 1 inch past the beginning end of the strip. Turn the end under and wrap it around the beginning end. Continue serging the strip in place.

5. Press binding away from the quilt top.

6. Turn the quilt over with the backing side up. Apply fusible web tape along the binding fold, following the manufacturer's instructions. Remove the paper backing and fold the binding down to just cover the stitching line. Fuse in place.

Tips for Success

A specialty foot, sometimes called a stitch-in-the-ditch foot or an edge-joining foot, has a center guide in front of the needle that makes it a perfect tool for quilting in the ditch. Just keep the guide riding in the seam as you sew, and your stitches will be tucked in the seam perfectly. Check your owner's manual, machine dealer or sewing-supply catalog for availability for your sewing machine.

74

7. Using sewing machine with invisible thread in the needle and bobbin thread to match the binding, stitch in the binding seamline on the front of the quilt, catching the folded edge on the back in the stitching. ❖

Credits: Michael Miller Gypsy Blossom collection fabrics; Pellon® Shape-Flex woven fusible interfacing; Fairfield Processing Corp. Cotton Classic batting; Warm Company Steam-a-Seam 2® fusible web tape.

Bordered Tablecloth With Ruffle

Designer's Notes

Put some pizzazz in your family's mealtime with this pretty bordered tablecloth that is not only fast to make with a serger but easy too! The ruffle has rolled edges and is gathered by flat locking over pearl cotton—a fun technique to add to your serger skills. To make your tablecloth larger or smaller, adjust the center measurement, and shorten or lengthen the borders accordingly. The border depth and corner squares will remain the same size.

Serger Skill Level

Intermediate

Finished Size

60 x 86 inches

Serger Skills

Flat-lock gathering, rolled edges, 4-thread overcast stitching

Materials

- 44/45-inch-wide 100-percent cotton fabrics:
  - 2 yards print *(A)*
  - 2 yards coordinating print *(B)*
  - ⅝ yard coordinating print *(C)*
  - ⅜ yard coordinating print *(D)*
- Self-adhesive, double-sided basting tape
- Basic sewing supplies and equipment

Threads

- 4 cones coordinating serger thread
- 1 cone pearl cotton serger thread
- All-purpose coordinating sewing thread

Serger Stitches & Settings

Note: *These are suggested serger settings. Be sure to test your stitch on a scrap of project or similar fabric to ensure stitch perfection before beginning your project.*

4-thread wide overlock for seams & edges

Stitch Length: 2.5
Left Needle Tension: 6
Right Needle Tension: 4
Upper Looper Tension: 4
Lower Looper Tension: 4

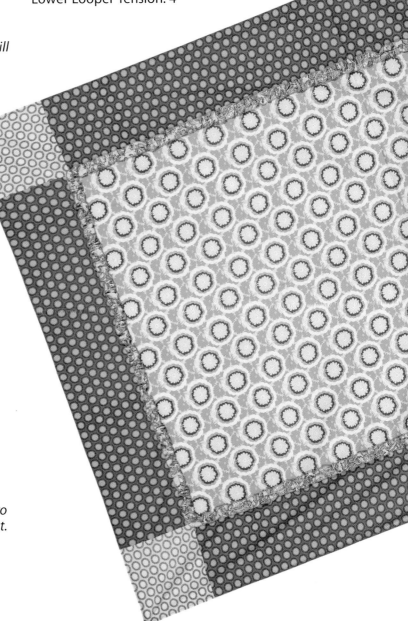

3-thread rolled edge for ruffle
Stitch Length: 1.0
Left Needle: Removed
Right Needle Tension: 4
Upper Looper Tension: 3
Lower Looper Tension: 6

3-thread flat lock for gathering
Stitch Length: 3.0
Left Needle Tension: 1
Right Needle: Removed
Upper Looper Tension: 3
Lower Looper Tension: 6

Optional for flat locking on fold: Foot to protect fabric from cutting blade, if available, or disengage cutting blade, referring to your owner's manual.

Machine Threading
Coordinating serger thread in both needles and loopers.

Cutting
From print fabric A:
Cut one 43 x 69-inch rectangle the lengthwise grain of the fabric for tablecloth center.

From coordinating print fabric B:
Cut two 10 x 43-inch end borders the lengthwise grain of the fabric.

Cut two 10 x 69-inch side borders the lengthwise grain of the fabric.

From coordinating print fabric C:
Cut 10 strips 1¾-inch-wide by fabric width, cutting on the cross grain for the ruffles.

From coordinating print fabric D:
Cut four 10 x 10-inch squares for border corners.

Assemble Tablecloth
Stitch seams with right sides together using a ½-inch seam allowance.

1. Using the suggested 4-thread overlock, serge the 10 x 69-inch side borders to the long sides of the tablecloth center.

2. Serge one 10-inch square to both 10-inch edges of the two 10 x 43-inch end borders.

3. Serge the end borders to the center/side borders piece.

4. Finish the edges of the assembled tablecloth with the suggested 4-thread overlock.

5. Press under a ½-inch hem and topstitch with the sewing machine.

Assemble Ruffle
1. Serge the short edges of the 10 fabric C strips together to make a continuous ruffle strip. Press seams to one side.

2. Set the serger for a 3-thread rolled edge and finish both long edges of the ruffle strip.

3. Press the ruffle strip in half lengthwise with right sides together.

4. Set the serger for a 3-thread flat lock and disengage the blade, referring to your owner's manual. If you cannot disengage the blade, be careful to keep the fabric clear of the blade.

5. Align pearl cotton thread with the center fold and flat lock along the fold with half the stitch width extending beyond the fold, encasing the pearl cotton thread in the stitching (Figure 1).

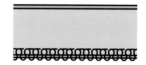

Figure 1

6. Open the ruffle and press.

7. Secure one end of the pearl cotton thread to the ruffle fabric. Pull the pearl cotton thread to gather the ruffle strip to 220 inches; knot the pearl cotton thread to secure and trim extra. Evenly distribute the gathers.

8. Mark the ruffle into 42-inch and 68-inch sections as shown in Figure 2 to match the tablecloth sides.

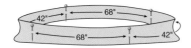

Figure 2

Finishing the Tablecloth

1. Place the tablecloth right side up on a large, flat surface.

2. Apply a strip of basting tape over the border seams (Figure 3); do not remove the backing.

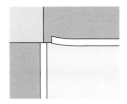

Figure 3

3. Working with one border seam at a time, remove the paper backing from the basting tape. Adhere the center of the ruffle strip firmly to the basting tape. Match the ruffle marking pins to the corners of the tablecloth border seams, adjusting ruffles if necessary (Figure 4).

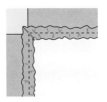

Figure 4

4. Use the sewing machine to stitch the center of the ruffle strip in place. ❖

Credits: *Amy Butler Soul Blossoms fabric collection from Westminster Fibers; Collins Wonder Tape basting tape; Coats & Clark serger and pearl cotton threads.*

Tip for Success

To adjust the ruffle length for another size, measure the perimeter of the center panel; then cut and piece a strip of fabric that is 1.5 to 2 times the perimeter length.

METRIC CONVERSION CHARTS

Metric Conversions

Canada/U.S. Measurement		Multiplied by		Metric Measurement
yards	x	.9144	=	metres (m)
yards	x	91.44	=	centimetres (cm)
inches	x	2.54	=	centimetres (cm)
inches	x	25.40	=	millimetres (mm)
inches	x	.0254	=	metres (m)

Canada/U.S. Measurement		Multiplied by		Metric Measurement
centimetres	x	.3937	=	inches
metres	x	1.0936	=	yards

Standard Equivalents

Canada/U.S. Measurement		Metric Measurement			Canada/U.S. Measurement		Metric Measurement		
⅛ inch	=	3.20 mm	=	0.32 cm	1⅜ yards	=	125.73 cm	=	1.26 m
¼ inch	=	6.35 mm	=	0.635 cm	1½ yards	=	137.16 cm	=	1.37 m
⅜ inch	=	9.50 mm	=	0.95 cm	1⅝ yards	=	148.59 cm	=	1.49 m
½ inch	=	12.70 mm	=	1.27 cm	1¾ yards	=	160.02 cm	=	1.60 m
⅝ inch	=	15.90 mm	=	1.59 cm	1⅞ yards	=	171.44 cm	=	1.71 m
¾ inch	=	19.10 mm	=	1.91 cm	2 yards	=	182.88 cm	=	1.83 m
⅞ inch	=	22.20 mm	=	2.22 cm	2⅛ yards	=	194.31 cm	=	1.94 m
1 inches	=	25.40 mm	=	2.54 cm	2¼ yards	=	205.74 cm	=	2.06 m
⅛ yard	=	11.43 cm	=	0.11 m	2⅜ yards	=	217.17 cm	=	2.17 m
¼ yard	=	22.86 cm	=	0.23 m	2½ yards	=	228.60 cm	=	2.29 m
⅜ yard	=	34.29 cm	=	0.34 m	2⅝ yards	=	240.03 cm	=	2.40 m
½ yard	=	45.72 cm	=	0.46 m	2¾ yards	=	251.46 cm	=	2.51 m
⅝ yard	=	57.15 cm	=	0.57 m	2⅞ yards	=	262.88 cm	=	2.63 m
¾ yard	=	68.58 cm	=	0.69 m	3 yards	=	274.32 cm	=	2.74 m
⅞ yard	=	80.00 cm	=	0.80 m	3⅛ yards	=	285.75 cm	=	2.86 m
1 yard	=	91.44 cm	=	0.91 m	3¼ yards	=	297.18 cm	=	2.97 m
1⅛ yards	=	102.87 cm	=	1.03 m	3⅜ yards	=	308.61 cm	=	3.09 m
1¼ yards	=	114.30 cm	=	1.14 m	3½ yards	=	320.04 cm	=	3.20 m
					3⅝ yards	=	331.47 cm	=	3.31 m
					3¾ yards	=	342.90 cm	=	3.43 m
					3⅞ yards	=	354.32 cm	=	3.54 m
					4 yards	=	365.76 cm	=	3.66 m
					4⅛ yards	=	377.19 cm	=	3.77 m
					4¼ yards	=	388.62 cm	=	3.89 m
					4⅜ yards	=	400.05 cm	=	4.00 m
					4½ yards	=	411.48 cm	=	4.11 m
					4⅝ yards	=	422.91 cm	=	4.23 m
					4¾ yards	=	434.34 cm	=	4.34 m
					4⅞ yards	=	445.76 cm	=	4.46 m
					5 yards	=	457.20 cm	=	4.57 m

Special thanks to Edwards Sewing Center of Fort Wayne, Indiana, (www.edwardssewing.com) for providing sergers for this book.

Annie's® *Serger Sewing Basics* is published by Annie's, 306 East Parr Road, Berne, IN 46711. Printed in USA. Copyright © 2011, 2013 Annie's. All rights reserved. This publication may not be reproduced in part or in whole without written permission from the publisher.

RETAIL STORES: If you would like to carry this pattern book or any other Annie's publications, visit AnniesWSL.com

Every effort has been made to ensure that the instructions in this pattern book are complete and accurate. We cannot, however, take responsibility for human error, typographical mistakes or variations in individual work. Please visit AnniesCustomerCare.com to check for pattern updates.

ISBN: 978-1-59217-364-8

5 6 7 8 9

Photo Index

35

38

41

44

46

52

56

65

69

75